CONSTELLATIONS

Like the future itself, the imaginative possibilities of science fiction are limitless. And the very development of cinema is inextricably linked to the genre, which, from the earliest depictions of space travel and the robots of silent cinema to the immersive 3D wonders of contemporary blockbusters, has continually pushed at the boundaries. **Constellations** provides a unique opportunity for writers to share their passion for science fiction cinema in a book-length format, each title devoted to a significant film from the genre. Writers place their chosen film in a variety of contexts – generic, institutional, social, historical – enabling **Constellations** to map the terrain of science fiction cinema from the past to the present… and the future.

> 'This stunning, sharp series of books fills a real need for authoritative, compact studies of key science fiction films. Written in a direct and accessible style by some of the top critics in the field, brilliantly designed, lavishly illustrated and set in a very modern typeface that really shows off the text to best advantage, the volumes in the **Constellations** series promise to set the standard for SF film studies in the 21st century.'
> **Wheeler Winston Dixon, Ryan Professor of Film Studies, University of Nebraska**

 Constellations

 Constelbooks

Also available in this series

12 Monkeys Susanne Kord

Blade Runner Sean Redmond

Brainstorm Joseph Maddrey

Children of Men Dan Dinello

Close Encounters of the Third Kind Jon Towlson

The Damned Nick Riddle

Dune Christian McCrea

Ex Machina Joshua Grimm

Inception David Carter

Jurassic Park Paul Bullock

Lost Brigid Cherry

Mad Max Martyn Conterio

RoboCop Omar Ahmed

Rollerball Andrew Nette

Stalker Jon Hoel

Forthcoming

Mr. Freedom Tyler Sage

The OA David Sweeney

The Stepford Wives Samantha Lindop

CONSTELLATIONS

Seconds

Jez Conolly & Emma Westwood

Acknowledgements

We would like to thank John Atkinson at Auteur/LUP for signing the trust instruments and giving us the opportunity to surgically dismantle, examine and reassemble this fine film. Thankfully, after being on the waiting list for quite a long time, post-operative complications were minimal. We would also like to express our deep gratitude to Salome Jens for offering her time and providing us with some fascinating memories of the production and experience of *Seconds*.

First published in 2021 by
Auteur, an imprint of Liverpool University Press,
4 Cambridge Street, Liverpool L69 7ZU
www.liverpooluniversitypress.co.uk/imprints/Auteur/
Copyright © Auteur 2021

Series design: Nikki Hamlett at Cassels Design
Set by Cassels Design www.casselsdesign.co.uk

All stills from Seconds © Joel Productions / John Frankenheimer Productions / Gibraltar Productions / Paramount Pictures

All rights reserved. No part of this publication may be reproduced in any material form (including photocopying or storing in any medium by electronic means and whether or not transiently or incidentally to some other use of this publication) without the permission of the copyright owner.

British Library Cataloguing-in-Publication Data
A catalogue record for this book is available from the British Library

ISBN paperback: 978-1-80085-929-6
ISBN hardback: 978-1-80085-928-9
ISBN epub: 978-1-80085-809-1
ISBN PDF: 978-1-80085-849-7

Contents

FIRSTS: 'Ah, there you are, Mr. Wilson. Come in. Please' 7

SECONDS: 'Begin again, all new, all different' 19

MEMORY: 'Well you see, it all began with a big red ball' 35

ARTIST | SURGEON: 'You were my best work' 45

SKIN | MEAT | FLUID: 'Sure you don't want this chicken?' 61

SEX | DRUGS | ROCK | PAPER | SCISSORS: 'There's a kind of gathering...
It's going to be very wild' 75

SOUND | VISION: 'Of course, the photography is not too professional...
but I think it's clear enough' 89

WORK | CONSUME | DIE: 'The years I've spent, trying to get all the
things I was told were important, that I was supposed to want' 101

LASTS: 'Relax, old friend. Cranial drill' 113

Bibliography 115

FIRSTS: 'Ah, there you are, Mr Wilson. Come in. Please'

"If you're going to write a song, try to get together with a collaborator because it's better to write with collaborators." – *Brian Wilson*

In his 1991 autobiography, *Wouldn't it be Nice: My Own Story*, the leader and co-founder of the Beach Boys, Brian Wilson, explained the effect that entering a movie theatre midway through a screening of *Seconds* (1966) had on him. We should bear in mind that, at the time of recalling and writing his account of the incident, Wilson was still firmly under the micromanagement of his ethically dubious psychotherapist Eugene Landy. Added to which, and by his own admission, at the time of his exposure to the film he was also in the midst of a period of particularly severe paranoid delusions fuelled by a cocktail of drugs and the pressure to write and produce, so we should take his account with a pinch of salt. However, according to his memoir, Wilson returned home from the cinema one December night in 1966 to be met by his associates and houseguests in a state of agitated shock and terror:

> I explained that I'd gone to the movies and asked if anyone had seen the Rock Hudson movie. None had. But [*Saturday Evening Post* music critic Jules] Seigel knew the story, which concerned a businessman who, frustrated with his life,

undergoes reconstructive surgery and acquires a new identity. Despite the change, he still finds himself fighting the same conflicts. I found it most similar to my life, frighteningly so.

"I walked into that movie and the first thing that happened was a voice from the screen said 'Hello, Mr. Wilson.' It completely blew my mind. You've got to admit that's pretty spooky, right?"

"The whole thing was in the movie," I ranted as if I could make them understand by the force and volume of my explanation. "My whole life. Birth and death and rebirth. The whole thing. Even the beach was in it, a whole thing about the beach. It was my whole life right there on screen." (Wilson/Gold 1991: 157-158)

Later in the autobiography, Wilson confesses, as a result of this traumatic experience, he did not set foot in a cinema again for another 16 years, at which point he felt able to witness a screening of *E.T. the Extra-Terrestrial* (Steven Spielberg, 1982). History does not record the effect that watching the Spielberg film had on the reclusive songwriter. What *is* known, however, is that around the time of his paranoid brush with *Seconds*, Wilson abandoned his work on *Smile*, the projected follow-up album to the Beach Boys' *Pet Sounds* that was released in the May of 1966. *Smile* came to be regarded as one of the great unreleased albums in the history of popular music. It would eventually resurface after a fashion as the reinterpreted solo album *Brian Wilson presents Smile* in 2011.

Coincidentally, *Seconds* has spent a great deal of that same intervening period filed away from the public gaze, initially due to a particularly negative critical reception that severely truncated its first theatrical run, and subsequently thanks to rather limited availability as a commercial home video or DVD title. In the US, certainly, this issue of restricted exposure was resolved with Criterion's August 2013 restored DVD release of *Seconds* in the director's preferred aspect ratio of 1.75:1, as well as, in the UK, the October 2015 release of the film as a two-disc dual format Blu-ray and DVD in Eureka Entertainment's Masters of Cinema series.[1]

Some would argue that a book about a film should work for the reader even if he or she has not seen the film before reading the book. But given the cult reputation of

Seconds, it is a moderately safe bet that if you possess this book you do so because its focus is a film that you are already aware of, have probably seen before, and one that you are curious to learn more about. So consequently much of what follows assumes at least an entry level degree of familiarity with the subject. There will be a little exposition coming up but, frankly, if you have read this far and simply have not seen the film previously, you would be well advised to stop right here, seek out a viewing copy as a matter of urgency, sit down, watch it and then come back to this point.

So, to proceed: if ever a film deserves a second life, it is *Seconds*, director John Frankenheimer's criminally overlooked monolith of bleak paranoia. Part science-fiction-of-the-speculative-present persuasion, part proto-body-horror, part noir-thriller-cum-black-comedy, a film that is locatable at the thematic and stylistic intersection of the post-McCarthy mindset, European art cinema, the suburban identity nightmares of *The Twilight Zone* and the mid-life crises of malehood aroused by 1960s counterculture. *Seconds* is a film that pushes into parallel definitions and bullheadedly refuses to be described in 25 words or less. So in the spirit of endeavour, here are in excess of 35,000 that will try.

A culmination of its director's 'Paranoia trilogy' commentary on the State of the Nation – it was preceded by *The Manchurian Candidate* in 1962 and *Seven Days in May* in 1964 – *Seconds* features a Hollywood star in the form of Rock Hudson at the height of his popularity and garnered an Academy Award nomination for its cinematographer, James Wong Howe. Yet, for all its eclectic centrality, *Seconds* has dwelt in a collective blind spot for much of its life cycle. Arguably the bleakest mainstream Hollywood film ever made, it was roundly booed at the 1966 Cannes Film Festival and was a commercial failure upon release. Over time, the film's critical reception has gradually turned to acknowledge its significance in the grand scheme of American cinema, and among the cult circuit cognoscenti it has certainly earned its stripes, but throughout the wider science fiction cinema community it remains for many surprisingly unseen.

Placing *Seconds* in an exclusively science fiction cinema context is a little problematic. Many of the key films in the genre made during the decade and a half that preceded *Seconds*' release are regularly characterised and conjoined by their implied depiction of the paranoid fear of communism. *Invasion of the Body Snatchers* (Don Seigel, 1956), that touchstone text from the McCarthy years, is frequently held up as an exemplar of this, although that film's coincidental ambiguity allows for an opposing reading or simply an appreciation of the fundamental fear of the loss of liberty and any form of social control. Other science fiction films from the era explored the literal destructiveness and existential threat posed by atomic then nuclear technology. The more fantastical post-apocalyptic depictions seen in films like *Day the World Ended* (Roger Corman, 1955) and *The World, the Flesh and the Devil* (Ranald MacDougall, 1959) gave way to grittier, more polemical treatments, such as can be seen in *The Day the Earth Caught Fire* (Val Guest, 1961) and *Dr. Strangelove or: How I stopped Worrying and Learned to Love the Bomb* (Stanley Kubrick, 1964), although the speculative fiction element of the latter is more than matched by its satirical black comedy.

A significant influence on *Seconds* preceded it by ten years and can be found outside the genre. *The Man in the Grey Flannel Suit* (Nunnally Johnson, 1956), based on the hit 1955 novel of the same name written by Sloan Wilson, struck a chord, and perhaps a nerve, among America's middle class, male white-collar workforce with its story of the prototypical discontented businessman and the strain of executive conformity. It encapsulated a particular anxiety and through its drama raised the fundamental question on the mind of many a working man trapped in the mechanism of the American Dream: who am I? As the decades turned and the Cold War chilled, that managerial anxiety fused with the prevailing countercultural reaction to living in the shadow of the bomb and a fresh version of that question came to be asked: who do I want to be?

The timing of *Seconds* places it at the centre of that sociocultural fusion. However, the adjacency of the old and new attitudes in the second half of the 1960s produced a further development of this anxiety. The fear of personal erasure at the hands of an authoritative or manipulating system, rather than obliteration due to the technology of mass destruction, led to another iteration of the question: how do I know you're you, and I'm me? And so we have the dark distillation that is *Seconds*: the dissatisfaction of the invisible working man in a rapidly changing world, falling into a pact with the very system that enslaves him in an effort to free himself of the chains of mediocrity, only to discover that the freedom he has been promised is a mirage that commodifies his identity all the more, to the point of expedient erasure. The idea of the shadowy organisation controlling individuals without their knowledge would rapidly become a standard element of much science fiction cinema in the 1970s and 1980s, representing a growing awareness of and disaffection with ruthless, dehumanising capitalism. Think of the Spectacular Optical Corporation in *Videodrome* (David Cronenberg, 1983), Weyland-Yutani in *Aliens* (James Cameron, 1986) and Omni Consumer Products in *RoboCop* (Paul Verhoven, 1987) and you can see how the notion of the sinister corporation took off as the prevailing antagonist in the genre.

This book will consider Frankenheimer's film as both emblematic of the time in which it was made and perpetually relevant to new audiences as a portent of things to come, or for that matter a startling reveal of the hidden here and now. Arguably, the finest attribute of science fiction, both literary and cinematic, is its ability to reflect upon contemporary ideas and issues, and through a lens that consciously stretches plausibility and often employs allegory, offer a foretelling of the not-so-distant future. This attribute can also be its undoing. For some, the genre falls all too frequently into the territory of 'far-fetched'. For others, its intention to forewarn can interfere with their reception of the work purely as an entertainment. With this in mind, we can perhaps regard *Seconds* as a 'necessary entertainment'. Among the many brickbats thrown at it by critics, the film's personality disorder, if you will, leaves it falling between many stools. The counter argument portrays a picture that picks itself up and bestrides the gaps, turning its inner identity crisis from a vice into a virtue.

Brian Wilson's extreme reaction to seeing *Seconds* may be bizarre and even unique but it is also indicative of the potency of the film; a potency that this book will set out to explore. Apposite to the split personality of the subject matter, that exploration will be 'dual personal' and subjective; a Frankenstein-like (perhaps *Frankenheimer-like*?) surgical stitching of the words of its two writers into the one inseparable and irreversible whole.

We wrote this book having come to the film through different circumstances. For one of us, reaching the age of 50 during the course of preparing and writing what you are now reading, it was an experience not unlike the central character of Arthur

Hamilton in the film, played by the-then 50-year-old John Randolph. Nowadays, just like Hamilton, this writer commutes to work between the centre of a big city and a quieter, leafier locale. When watching *Seconds* now compared to a first exposure nearly three decades ago, the thoughts it provokes feel very pertinent to present day. Not that turning 50 has initiated a phase of life when surgical rejuvenation is in any way an attractive proposition. It is simply that, if there is an age-related corner that a person, particularly a man, might turn, there has been something in the writer's own experience that gave him reason to pause, take stock, look back then forward, possessed as a result of a more informed understanding of the changing phases of life, together with a greater appreciation of mortality. In other words – and to come clean – whereas some men might step upon the tumultuous crags of that semi-mythical realm known as the male menopause or the mid-life crisis and launch themselves headlong into a sad turmoil of youth-recapturing behaviour, he instead co-wrote this book.

The other writer, one born of a later decade, of the 'other' gender (in a binary sense) and an Antipodean world away (Australia) first viewed *Seconds* in her thirties and was surprised by the film's ability to fly outside her radar as a film aficionado, particularly a film of such obvious mastery that involved a mighty contingent of Hollywood talent. *Seconds*' unceremonious burial is almost as interesting as the film itself. Unpick it in the context of its mid-1960s American socio-political zeitgeist and a number of threads unravel that evidentially sent *Seconds* to an early grave. Throw in Hollywood's much-loved (and closeted) golden boy, Rock Hudson, and you have a film that defies the motherhood and apple pie of American Family Values. For this author, to know *Seconds* is to fully understand a fascinating and important cultural cataclysm that occurred in the mid-20th century, one that took place before she was born. *Seconds* acts as a capsule distillation of this seismic shift, in which patriarchy in all its guises – political, corporate and social – experienced its own mid-life crisis and, as a result, the very pillars of society became noticeably unstable. *Seconds* stabbed right at the heart of this raw paranoia but cut too close to the bone for those who were already immersed in the middle of it by 1966. Audiences and critics were not ready for *Seconds*, and yet all the reasons that made it unpalatable on its release make it all the more remarkable now.

Being a consciously personal study, albeit one shaped by two people and two voices cosmetically fused together, this book is inevitably and unapologetically subjective, so there is something to note at the outset: without wishing to induce an existential crisis in the reader, the tone, structure and nature of the book takes its cue to some extent from that of the film. *Seconds* is an illusory, complex and challenging piece of cinema whose central character is surgically disintegrated and reassembled into something new. It is a film consciously designed to unsettle the viewer via brutal dissection, exposure, reconstitution and destruction, so any book about *Seconds* would fail to do its source material justice if it did not also confront its audience through its choices of construction and discourse. Expect a loose collation of themes chosen from across the *Seconds* spectrum, and a somewhat fragmentary, visceral order of play based more on connections made and feelings triggered than on chronology of plot, pre-history or production schedule.

As a cumulative result of its discursive scatter, the commentary will resolve to establish a broad recognition of the film as a dark star in the science fiction film firmament, one that over the years since its production has proved hard for some to find, and once found continues to be hard for some to watch. It can certainly be said that *Seconds* is a film that, despite its public reputation, has heavily influenced the work of several subsequent highly regarded filmmakers. David Fincher's 1997 film *The Game* betrays many elements that one can find in the Frankenheimer film, and *Parasite* (2019) director Bong Joon-ho selected *Seconds* for a screening as part of 'The Bong Show', a January 2020 season of screenings of his own films alongside 'a carte blanche of favourite films handpicked by the director himself'. Another major devotee of the film is Christopher Nolan. In a 2006 interview with Philip Horne for the *Daily Telegraph*, around the time of release of the British director's film *The Prestige* (somewhat appropriately perhaps his own most overlooked film) Nolan had this to say:

> It's got a great audience hook, the idea of a man who is offered a second chance, who can escape into the freedom of another life. But Frankenheimer takes the story in another direction. For me, there's something very extreme about the pacing, something very, very slow and deliberate, very unexpected. *Seconds* simply doesn't make any concessions...[it] is very ominous the first time you watch

it – its whole style is very foreboding, and just builds through the whole movie. The second time you see it, when you know where it's going, it becomes really quite unbearable at times. (Horne 2006)

It remains a reservoir of inspiration, yet for Frankenheimer it never escaped its negative pigeonhole during his lifetime. Later parts of this study will explore the effect that it had on his career.

Certain overarching ideas and features will inevitably assert themselves repeatedly throughout the coming sections. The extent of the reconstructive surgery that features in the film may have been technically achievable in 1966, although perhaps barely imaginable to many at the time, which may explain why contemporary audiences found the central conceit of the film hard to swallow. It certainly predicted the rise of extreme cosmetic surgery and body modification that Western society would embrace in subsequent decades. In the context of the film, the lengthy procedures that convert the overweight, middle-aged Scarsdale, New York banker, Arthur Hamilton (played by Randolph), into the handsome, reclusive Malibu-Beach-located artist Tony Wilson (played by Hudson) say less about the narcissistic whims of the affluent and more about the ability of the system, represented in the film by 'the Company', to control and manipulate the individual. The post-surgical sutures that knit together the skin of Hamilton/Wilson become the strings that the Company puppet masters use to control their 'client'.

The allegory of the plasticity, puncturing and manipulation of skin will initiate a significant part of this study. This metaphor is set up and illuminated from the outset by the opening sequence, designed by Saul and Elaine Bass, which pulls aspects of the human face through the distortions of a dark and frightening funhouse mirror effect. Howe's camerawork similarly employs a variety of skewed angles, disorientating lenses and curiously destabilising camera mountings; the opening Grand Central Station sequence, in particular, moves between jerky hand-held and 'drunken' harness-mounted shots to achieve its effect. Several other scenes extend this notion; before entering into his transaction with the Company, the bewildered Hamilton is led through a (perhaps rather heavily) metaphorical meat-processing factory replete with rows of suspended cow carcasses. The permissive mass grape-treading sequence in the middle of the film, during which Wilson's inhibitions are broken down, is an extended bricolage of in-the-thick-of-it focal flukes, dizzying 'home movie' vérité and the orgiastic splashing of grape juice on the lens, and in so being both encapsulates the skin-rending plot themes and visuals, and also signifies the crush-processing of mere mortals under the foot of the Company.

These instances of extrusion and disruption build to suggest that the film stock, the very 'skin' of the film itself and/or the screen or the surface upon which one is viewing it, is being manipulated and pulled out of shape. Wong Howe's extra wide lensing could also be considered as a dimension under pressure, like lava between tectonic plates or, in the era of *Seconds*, the point where a previously dominant establishment and marauding counterculture collide and contort; squashed, distorted and uncomfortably buttressed against one another.

The political symbolism of the film will occupy a section of the book. There is a broad anti-establishment polemic at work in *Seconds*, broader than that employed by Frankenheimer in *The Manchurian Candidate and Seven Days in May*, both of which grounded themselves ostensibly in real-world geopolitical machinations. The point of *Seconds* is much more fundamental. Through its bleak, subjective eye, it seeks to illustrate the perils of the individual entering into a pact with the system – *Faust* by way of Kafka. As we have indicated, the representation of the Company as a shadowy corporate puppet master prefigures a science fiction film trope that will be familiar to many fans of the genre. As Murray Pomerance identified in his book *A Little Solitaire: John Frankenheimer and American Film*:

> *Seconds* can also be seen as an interesting precursor to the more prominent cycle of science fiction/horror films that emerged in the late 1970s-1980s, with the likes of *Demon Seed* (Donald Cammell 1977), *Alien* (Ridley Scott, 1979), and *The Terminator* (James Cameron, 1984). Turning a critical eye on the dehumanizing power of the corporation was to become the province of this later cycle of films, in which the human protagonists struggle to retain their selfhood as the cold logic of the corporate machine asserts its control...this struggle is played out upon bodies that are violently probed, penetrated, lacerated and technologically reconstituted. (Pomerance 2011: 231)

Given the comparative blind spot in which *Seconds* dwells, we have drawn explicit comparisons to several other more well-known films through the chapters in order to illustrate either *Seconds*' similarity, or in some instances its stark difference. Many of these comparator films were made in the same decade as *Seconds*, so this correlative practice serves doubly as a temporal locator, helping to place *Seconds* within the chronology of 1960s cinema.

This being principally a reflective response to the film rather than any kind of detailed 'director's diary' that charts the process of its making, we have consciously contained any such discussion, but a further condensed introduction to the themes that this book appraises can be found in the film's prehistory. It was based on the 1963 novel *Seconds* written by David Ely, published by Pantheon, the rights being acquired by Kirk Douglas and producer Edward Lewis for the sum of $75,000 with the intention that it would form the inaugural project of their new company Douglas and Lewis Productions. It was heralded in the January 1964 trade papers, the clear intention being that Douglas would play the lead. Douglas, who had worked with Frankenheimer on *Seven Days in May*, was quoted describing the film in critic A. H. Weiler's 'Pictures and People' column for the *New York Times*:

> *Seconds* is a contemporary horror story dealing, basically, with what could happen if you could get a second chance at life. It has to do with an organization that arranges for people who want to escape their way of life to be listed as dead and then changes them, through plastic surgery and other means, into entirely different personalities. Philosophically, it points up the question whether these people really want a new life after all. (Douglas 1964)

Both Frankenheimer and Douglas were very keen to have the actor play both Arthur Hamilton and Tony Wilson, presumably in aging make-up as Hamilton (see John Huston's 1963 film *The List of Adrian Messenger* for several examples of Douglas under transformative latex) but by the time the production got the green light Douglas had moved on to other projects. Prompted by this enforced change of direction, the eventual decision to cast two different actors in the roles remains for many the film's most indigestible element, and yet through the eventual casting of Rock Hudson as Wilson the film ultimately gained a richer sub-commentary on concealment, artifice and orchestrated identity change in post-war Hollywood. We are fortunate to be able to include a reflective contribution from Salome Jens, Hudson's co-star in the film, who through interview was able to provide a unique insight into the experience of working on the film and playing alongside Hudson.

What happens to Hudson's character in his second life, and how he comes to realise too late the ruination of his first one, is the nub of the film's desperate potency. As he bitterly remarks to an old friend and fellow 'Reborn' in the film's final minutes:

> 'I had to find out where I went wrong. The years I've spent trying to get all the things I was told were important. That I was told to want. Things, not people or meaning, just things.'

Notes

1. Any readers interested in consuming a contrasting companion piece to this book would be well advised to take a listen to the excellent audio commentary available on this latter commercial release compiled and delivered by Adrian Martin, together with a read of the insightful mini-essay written by David Cairns and published in the disc's accompanying booklet. These disc extras were the pick of the crop, but there are many other excellent contributions to be found on both the Criterion and Eureka releases, so here are the special features listed in their entirety:

   (Criterion)
   - New 4K digital film restoration, with uncompressed monaural soundtrack
   - Audio commentary featuring director John Frankenheimer
   - Actor Alec Baldwin on Frankenheimer and *Seconds*
   - New program on the making of *Seconds*
   - Interview with Frankenheimer from 1971
   - New visual essay by film scholars R. Barton Palmer and Murray Pomerance
   - PLUS: An essay by critic David Sterritt

   (Eureka)
   - Gorgeous restoration from a 4K transfer, in 1080p HD on the Blu-ray
   - Two Feature-length audio commentaries: one by director John Frankenheimer, and one by film scholar Adrian Martin
   - New video interview with novelist and critic Kim Newman

- Optional English subtitles for the deaf and hearing-impaired
- Original theatrical trailer
- Booklet featuring new essays by critics David Cairns and Mike Sutton

SECONDS: 'Begin again, all new, all different'

> We will never take unnecessary risks or compromise on our quality of our staff and service. We are always there for you each step of the way through your patient journey, providing 24-hour support with your surgeon and ensuring your recovery is quick and without any complications. – *Taken from the 'Our Philosophy' section of a leading cosmetic surgery consultants' website*

As indicated, this study will confront and address a range of issues that *Seconds* provokes, so rather than devote the entire volume to a linear walk-through with plot points serving as road signs, we will begin with a condensed chronology then move on to a series of more subjective sections. *Seconds* is a film best recognised as a semi-hallucinatory experience, and so to aid that recognition, by way of a set of cognitive coordinates, this initial extended digest is provided partly to act as an *aide memoire* of story and also to introduce some naming conventions and terms of reference in order to avoid the repeated stating of details. So consider this a section to return to when subsequent reflections and connections veer towards the philosophical or abstract.

A word on the identity and naming of the central character: references to 'Arthur Hamilton' or just 'Hamilton' from hereon are associated with the pre-operative life of our protagonist, while instances of 'Tony Wilson' or plain 'Wilson' relate to the post-operative phase. You may find occasional references to 'Hamilton/Wilson' when discussion turns to subjects that pertain to both parts of the character's personality or the point being explored is focused on the transitional process between the two identities.

We shall dispense with regular occurrences of the post-surgical character's full given name, 'Antiochus Wilson', as it is mentioned in the film just three times, and only by Wilson himself when speaking in third person. He is much more routinely called 'Tony' by others. However, that is not to neglect the significance of the unusual alias 'Antiochus', being a somewhat regal identity bestowed on Hamilton as a Reborn, of which, as the client of the Company, he has no recourse. In David Ely's original novel

Seconds, as adapted by screenwriter Lewis John Carlino, Wilson objects to what he considers 'a terrible name to give a man' and is told by the Company representative: 'You'll get accustomed to it, sir. To my mind, it has a noble ring, if I may venture to say so. And besides, you are at liberty to use the diminutive "Tony", if you like, in daily affairs' (Ely 1963: 73).

Author Sean Easton, writing on the classical motifs in *Seconds*, aptly expounds on the symbolism of the 'Antiochus' title, and a 'title' it definitely could be considered, given the most notable Antiochuses of history were Hellenic Greek kings from the Seleucid empire. Most significantly for our purposes, Antiochus IV Epiphanes – the enemy of Jews according to *The Book of the Macabees* – introduced ancient society to the concept of 'the gymnasium', which saw many Jewish males disguising their circumcisions so as to blend into an environment where nudity was often on display and, consequently, their true identity compromised. As Easton writes:

> According to this view, Hellenic culture under Antiochus IV threatened Jewish culture not only through directly repressive measures but also indirectly by inciting males to alter the appearance of their bodies... It resonates with Hamilton/Wilson's own feeling that the name Antiochus signifies an alien entity to which he has surrendered himself.

Easton goes on to add:

> The appeal of a Hellenic identity to a non-Greek in the Seleucid empire of the second century B.C.E. may be imagined as similar in one respect to that of youth to an aging banker in 1960s America: each identity promises, in exchange for certain erasures of the self, access to a new life of privilege and opportunity. (Easton 2012: 203)

The fact that 'Antiochus Wilson' as a full name can be truncated to the innocuously Anglo-Saxon 'Tony Wilson' further cements this existential metaphor at play for the film's protagonist – an everyday, average white male caught in a fabled Greek Tragedy; at once Dionysian and Aesopian but also Faustian and Kafkaesque.

Seconds starts with visual abstraction that is tethered by text; the Saul and Elaine Bass opening credits constitute a blur of dark dissolves combined with a mix of stark, white upper- and lower-case Helvetica titles.[1] The font choice and use is similar to that found in the Bass-designed credits for *Psycho* (Alfred Hitchcock 1960), the difference being that, for the opening of the Hitchcock film, the letter forms fragment along hard linear plains creating a near-Op Art visual disturbance intended to convey the disintegration of the mind. What plays out behind the titles of *Seconds* is a distortion and disintegration of the *body*, or at least a sectional deformation of facial features; eyes, nose, mouth, ears warped out of shape and presented in nightmarishly fused cubist/surrealist combination as both a tonal and visual foretaste of the film. Reality will bend and stretch to breaking point. That visual tone is more than matched by Jerry Goldsmith's Neo-Baroque musical score, a *Danse Macabre*-derived soundtrack of jarring organ chords and shrill strings.

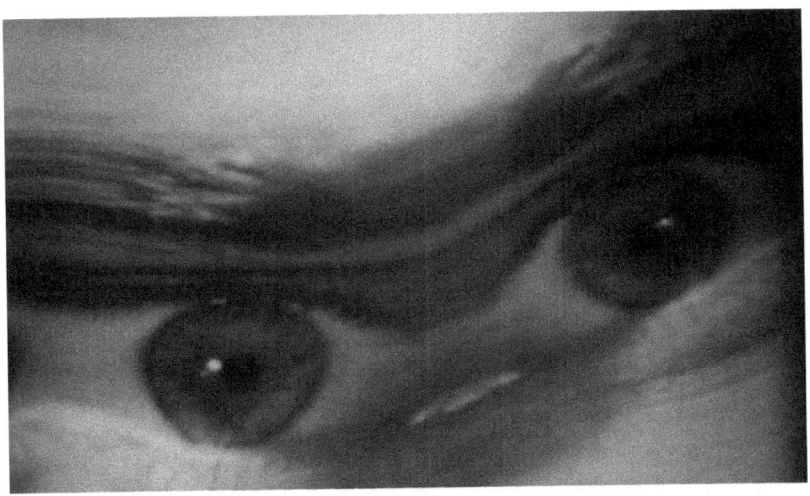

In their book studying the work of Saul Bass, Jennifer Bass and Pat Kirkham reveal the simple process behind this highly effective primer to the film's content. Art Goodman, the Bass' long-time collaborator, acted as the model whose reflection off aluminium sheets was photographed and then manipulated to create the distorted reality to 'symbolically set the stage for what was to come' according to Saul Bass; a perfect visual stitching with James Wong Howe's upcoming cinematography (Bass/Kirkham 2011).

This opening titles appetiser ends with a cropped portrait shot of a head almost entirely enclosed within sterile surgical dressing, mere slits cut for eyes, nostrils and mouth, and it is into this open mouth that we go, the quivering lips framing the final title 'directed by JOHN FRANKENHEIMER'. We close in on teeth linked visibly by thin, straight filaments of saliva, drawn perpendicular like tramline scratches in the emulsion of the film itself. In his Criterion Collection commentary, John Frankenheimer remarked on this opening title sequence:

> 'Have the audience feel right from the beginning that something was not what it should be; that this was not going to be a straightforward narrative film. And I think you get that from the titles, and we carry that into the first Grand Central Station sequence.'

The blur of the sequence dissolves into a balcony perspective of the main concourse at New York's Grand Central Terminal, the fluid bend of the picture resolving as the milling dark dots of commuters below. From this panoramic establishing shot, we cut to a tight close-up of another cropped portrait of a man's head; only hat, eyes, nose are in frame, and all to right of shot, with the ground level of the concourse as background. The man is walking through the crowd in some concealed pursuit, his steady stride pattern determining the editing pace of the assemblage of shots for the next two minutes of screen time. What is intercut among the cropped shots of the man's head could be described as angles from his *field* of view, certainly not his *point* of view; a mix of aspects from behind the man with the back of his head and his right shoulder in view, knee-high roaming shots angled upwards, all suggestive of an act of stalking surveillance.[2]

The focus of the pursuit quickly becomes apparent; a portly middle-aged man in a grey felt porkpie hat, his round, anxious face and vaguely weary demeanour symptomatic of the mantle of the eroded male breadwinner; middle-class, managerial, stressed, a mid-century stereotype of Western, especially American, society still prevalent at the time of the film's making. This is Arthur Hamilton, the New York banker making his way from office to domicile at the end of another working day, heading for train number 2046 leaving from Track 25 at 5.23pm, carrying briefcase, folded evening newspaper and the cares of the world. Hamilton makes the train, as does his pursuer, who has just enough time to attract Hamilton's attention and slap a small crumpled piece of paper into the palm of his hand before rapidly disembarking. The train moves off and Hamilton can only watch the stranger who knew him shrink back to become just another anonymous figure on the platform. The unexpected event clearly unnerves Hamilton; there is something in his clammy social discomfort, sitting among his fellow commuters holding this scrap of paper, which suggests that he is making a connection in his mind with another as-yet-unrevealed occurrence. On the crumpled note is written an address: 34 Lafayette Street.

Hamilton alights at Scarsdale station where his wife, Emily (Frances Reid),[3] collects him and drives him the short distance to their respectable suburban dwelling. The drive-home conversation is banal; roses out back trimmed, news of a letter received from their daughter, Sally; all received by Hamilton with an irritability that triggers Emily's concern. She broaches the matter of a phone call in the early hours, which Hamilton dismisses as 'just a crazy prank'. And yet, later, in the middle of the night, he waits anxiously by the telephone, the piece of paper passed to him on the train propped against the dial.

The telephone rings, Hamilton cups the handset to his ear:

'Art, it's me again... Charlie Evans!'

Hamilton is certain that his old friend and former tennis doubles partner at Princeton, Charlie Evans (ironically played by another Hamilton, actor Murray Hamilton, recognised by many as the mayor from *Jaws* [Steven Spielberg, 1975]), is dead. This doesn't even sound like Charlie but the voice on the end of the line implores Hamilton to walk the few steps to the mantlepiece, pick up a silver trophy and pull back one edge of the felt on its base.

'"Fidelis Eternis" – you scratched it there, down in the locker room after we won the final. Remember? With your belt buckle.'

One sight of the scratched phrase provides Hamilton with enough evidence that this is indeed Charlie Evans to whom he is speaking. Charlie desperately wants Arthur to experience the new life he has found.

> *'You've got to come tomorrow. Listen. If you don't show up, that's it. Think, for Pete's sake. What have you got now? What?'*

In terms of mid-20th century Western indicators, Hamilton has everything. Or does he? It doesn't *feel* like he has everything, if his demeanour was to indicate anything. The answer notwithstanding, Charlie persuades him to go to the Lafayette Street address just after noon the following day, and to use the name 'Wilson'.

Upon returning to bed after the telephone conversation, Hamilton is gently probed for information by Emily and, like the conversation in the car, his response is irritable and concealing. It's clear to his wife that he has something on his mind and she persuades him to make an appointment to see the family doctor. To ease his fevered state, she attempts some gestures of physical intimacy but Hamilton responds with libido-deflated stoniness. It plays out as an uncomfortable and wilfully unromantic scene in so many ways, James Wong Howe's camera capturing the forced pressing of their flesh in a sequence of jarring angles with harsh, unforgiving lighting. The moment passes. With lights out, Hamilton lies awake, staring at the bedroom ceiling.

As midday the following day approaches, Hamilton distractedly goes through the motions of dictating the contents of a letter declining a loan extension to his secretary at the bank, with one eye on his wristwatch. This seemingly banal interaction foreshadows that which he too will experience later in the film's narrative, although with Hamilton/Wilson himself assuming the role of the disempowered customer, an emotionally divested Company person delivering the rejection.

The Lafayette Street destination turns out to be a drab dry-cleaning establishment where, amid the steam, he is passed another piece of paper bearing the address of a slaughterhouse in the city's meat packing district. A taxi brings him to an abattoir: '"Honest Arnie": the Used Cow Dealer'[4] where he is immediately addressed as 'Mr. Wilson' and through which he is led, past the refrigerated rows of split, suspended cow carcasses, out to the rear of the building where he dazedly but dutifully accepts a ride in the back of a meat wagon. Hamilton has symbolically stepped onto the conveyer belt of a flesh processing production line, one that is not as far removed from the "Honest Arnie" dealership as he may originally think.

He emerges at some unknown location, an anonymous New York alley and a back-door delivery bay route to an elevator, which deposits him in a corridor possessing the blank décor of private medicine; that monetised hybrid of hospital and hospitality. A woman in a white nursing uniform appears and greets Hamilton:

'Ah Mr. Wilson, will you come this way please.'

She leads him from the corridor into the corporate health/wealth comfort of an office, complete with leather Chesterfield, bookcases, Picasso prints on the walls and a commanding executive's desk. Everything has an air of authoritative benevolence that would not seem out of place in Hamilton's Ivy League world, a soothing façade of institutionalised professionalism that masks something sinister. There's a cup of tea waiting for him in this office, which he obediently drinks, and as a consequence of the cup's contents he falls into drugged unconsciousness.[5]

His own torrid mauling of an unknown female plays through his opiated dream-state[6], and, with a start, Hamilton comes to and finds himself still sitting in the plush office. Returning consciousness brings with it an anxious desire to leave the premises. In seeking a way out, he happens upon a large room at the other end of the corridor filled with row upon row of men sitting at desks, writing, reading, crafting, variously occupied with an assortment of time-killing activities. One of the men stares at Hamilton, as if in recognition but, in returning the look, Hamilton doesn't reciprocate – this is the face of a stranger.

He is ushered back to the office where he meets Mr. Ruby (Jeff Corey) who initiates the reason for Hamilton's presence, the business transaction offered to him by the Company. For a not-insignificant payment, they will confect his demise, alter him surgically and provide him with a new life and all traces of his former self erased. This is a major reveal to us as the audience. Up until this point, we've been in the dark as to the motivation that has propelled Hamilton to the Company headquarters. In fact, we have travelled with him without even knowing the Company was our destination. Yet, like the confused Hamilton, we have still made the journey, drawn by a longbow of intrigue created by writer Lewis John Carlino.

'I've been assigned to go over the circumstances of your death with you.'

As an opening gambit in the discussion – a killer line, in all senses of the word – it should startle Hamilton but his response to Ruby's slick, casual patter is a progression from muted protest through stunned disquiet to word-fumbling acquiescence, suggesting Hamilton knows more than he has revealed to us. Ruby, the consultant-cum-salesman, calmly runs through the procedures and requirements. There is an incidental mention of 'CPS' – Cadaver Procurement Section – amid his matter-of-fact run-through of the cost factor involved ('in the neighbourhood of thirty thousand dollars') breezily skimmed over while he finger-picks through the chicken dinner that Hamilton has declined to eat – a particularly comical, innocuous gesture within an otherwise intensely grave moment.

A set of documents arrive for Hamilton to sign. His reluctance to do so triggers the screening of a short film depicting the rapacious events that he thought were just the figment of his earlier fever dream. It's a Company 'insurance policy' blackmail designed to guarantee Hamilton's signature. Left incredulous and open-mouthed by the footage, Hamilton finds himself alone in the office with 'the Old Man' (Will Geer) who, despite his easy manner, is clearly the big boss of the business. His soft words and orchestrated positioning steadily break down the remaining vestiges of Hamilton's resistance. The pen touches the paper, the scalpel touches the skin – it is a jump cut that propels us through a cosmetic surgery montage, which sees Arthur Hamilton 'reborn' as Antiochus 'Tony' Wilson, albeit swathed in surgical dressings.

 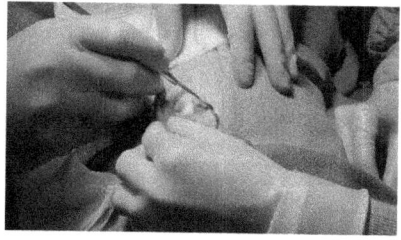

Healing begins and, before long, the bandages are removed. He who was Hamilton but is now Wilson overcomes the shock of seeing his new face for the first time and proceeds through post-operative therapy, both physical and psychological. This is the 'It's alive!' Frankenstein/Frankenheimer moment; John Randolph is now (miraculously) Rock Hudson and, as such, the character-matching begins whereby we are asked to suspend our belief and see these two very different actors as being one and the same. Thankfully, the calibre of their performances narrow the imaginative divide that the audience must leap.[7]

Wilson meets with Davalo (Khigh Dheigh), his 'guidance advisor', who plays back an audiotape of him recorded while he was under the influence of pentothal and caffeine sodium benzoate. The recording reveals Wilson's deepest basic, perhaps infantile desire: *'I guess I'd like to paint stuff...pictures and things'.*

It is on the basis of these regressions that the Company assembles Wilson's new life. He is to be an artist, based at a luxurious private studio in Malibu, California. He is a bachelor, what could be considered a fêted status for men of the 1960s, with the 'bachelor pad' presented as something of a male utopia.[8] As Davalo puts it:

> *'In short, you are alone in the world, absolved of all responsibility except to your own interest.'*

We next see Wilson, fully recovered and smartly suited, alone on a jet bound for Los Angeles International Airport. His skin has healed but he is not yet comfortable in it. A panic attack on the plane sees him rush to the on-board restroom and down some anti-anxiety pills. When exiting LAX, he encounters an excitable stranger who clearly recognises him, shouting his name across the terminal and seemingly providing Wilson with a capsule summation of his own new life. If the stranger's words are anything to go by, this Wilson is a man's man.

> *'Can't wait to get back to them pretty little models, huh? If I didn't have to catch a plane, I'd make you buy me a drink, by God!'*

Wilson is lost for words. Having been told he is alone in the world, the last thing he expected was to be greeted so ebulliently by an apparent acquaintance.

He arrives at his new beachfront residence and is greeted by John (Wesley Addy) who has been assigned by the Company to assist Wilson acclimatise to his new life. The property is bright and spacious with a private pool and, of course, an artist's studio already set up for Wilson to use.[9] Everything appears to have been thought of, and yet, despite the Company's care and attention, Wilson does not appear comfortable in these surroundings. He resists John's gentle but persistent encouragement to throw a cocktail party as a way to meet the other local residents, preferring instead to spend his time making very tentative stabs at painting and taking lonely walks along the shoreline.

On one such walk, he encounters Nora Marcus (Salome Jens)[10] – a neighbour, freethinker and fellow loner who, seemingly unprompted, takes an interest in him. They walk together then take tea back at her beach house where she reads both his tealeaves and his face: *'Somewhere in the man is still a key unturned'*.

Her flower child ruminations – which act as an awakening for the conservative Hamilton/Wilson to American counterculture – would appear to leave Wilson feeling that Nora is some kind of kindred spirit, perhaps a person who he could comfortably spend time with in this different, difficult, all-bought-and-paid-for existence, or at least somebody who might help him to turn that key. But, just like John, could she have been placed in his path by the Company simply to ease the passage into his new life?

He decides to join Nora at a gathering the following day along the coast at Santa Barbara. This scene – one of the most important in the film – will be further expounded upon later in this book in recognition of its significance but, in the meantime, we can observe that Nora's foretelling – *'It's going to be very wild'* – is a prophecy the Reborn Wilson/Hamilton hybrid could not fully comprehend.

The event is a Feast of Bacchus grape stomp party, a California wine country tradition but, this being the fall before the Summer of Love, it takes on major Sun Worshipper dimensions. There is a raucous and shambolically unravelling version of 'What Shall We Do with the Drunken Sailor?' played on pan pipes, tambourines, guitars and trumpets; wreaths of vine leaves are worn on heads; large quantities of grapes are tossed with abandon into the drum of the wine press, and soon clothes are shed as the partygoers embark upon their mass tread.

Wilson is initially deeply uncomfortable with the merry-making mayhem and, when Nora slips off her dress and joins the revellers in the wine press, he makes to extricate her but is unceremoniously stripped and bundled in too. Surrounded by the whirl of cacophonous intoxication, he struggles and splutters in an effort to avoid submersion in the rising juice but the baptism of wine begins to work and, like the grapes under foot, his skin of inhibition is broken down. He explodes in an orgasmic climax of euphoria, embracing Nora and, in that moment of freedom, finding out a little of what it really means to be Tony Wilson – or perhaps something that was always inside Arthur Hamilton.

Emboldened by the experience and what feels like the beginning of a beautiful friendship with Nora, Wilson throws the cocktail party for his neighbours at his house that John had been pressing him to arrange. The drink flows and soon Wilson is intoxicated to the point where Nora attempts to rein him in a little. She succeeds temporarily but Wilson continues to drink and, in a conversation about Harvard with a guest, he 'goes off-message' and lets slips that he, as in Arthur Hamilton, also went to Harvard. He loudly and drunkenly sings lines from the university march song 'Harvardiana', attracting the attention of other guests in the process.

As he rapidly loses his remaining inhibitions, he even blurts out the name 'Arthur Hamilton', at which point he is lifted off his feet by several male partygoers, accompanied by John, and carried into the bedroom. He continues to let slip about his former life as Hamilton. There's mention of his nephew at Harvard, and also his daughter and the fact that he, Hamilton, might be a grandfather by now.

'Why are you all staring at me like that?'

Surrounded and pinned to the bed by these men, a cold bolt of sobriety strikes him. As the deadly serious faces of the men crowd over him, John loosens Wilson's tie and explains:

'They know. They're like you. Reborns.'

Nora bursts into the room in a rage at Wilson's conduct, and the full realisation of his infringement of the Company small print rules hits home.

The party's over. Alone in the house, Wilson receives a phone call from old pal Charlie, during which he learns that Nora is indeed not a Reborn but a company employee. With his feelings for her dashed, his new life is exposed as a sham. As if he didn't know that anyway.

Charlie urges him to stay put in Malibu and wait for the Company to send somebody out to help him through these early stages of his life-swap but we next see Wilson rushing back through LAX, evading the pursuit of some of the Reborns from the party as he flies back to New York. The Arthur Hamilton still very much inside Tony Wilson feels compelled to return to his Scarsdale family home, where he successfully passes himself off to his 'widow' as a friend of the supposedly now-deceased Hamilton. On the pretext of collecting one of Hamilton's watercolour paintings as a keepsake, he probes Emily to try to piece together a picture of her dead husband/his former self from her perspective. What he gathers offers little comfort. Even if he were able to reverse the process he has undergone, it would seem that she has moved on:

> *'He was a quiet man. The thing I most remember him for were his silences. It was as if he were always listening to something inside, some voice. He never talked about it, so I never knew what it was. He was a good man but he lived as if he were a stranger here.'*

Wilson departs, armed not with an Arthur Hamilton watercolour – Emily clearly hasn't kept any – but with just one remaining memento: the silver *Fidelis Eternis* tennis trophy. The irony of this Latin inscription is emphasised in the coming scenes when we learn that Hamilton's tennis buddy, Charlie, has not been entirely 'eternally faithful' but readily sold their friendship to save his own skin. What is eternity when you have cashed in one life for another? Does it remain binding in the next existence? And even the next? Obviously, the terms of this Charlie-Arthur *Fidelis Eternis* are very sketchy.

Outside the house after the visit, Wilson is collected by John in a Company car. He expresses his wish to go back, not to California but to the Company headquarters, figuring that, as they did before for Arthur Hamilton, they can now arrange Tony Wilson's 'death' so he can begin again, again. But there's a hitch – back at the Company office, Ruby presses him to recommend and sponsor a new client:

> *'As you can imagine, our business is acquired through present clients. It's a word-of-mouth operation, Wilson. You don't suppose we can advertise in magazines and newspapers... You were sponsored yourself, you know.'*

Wilson tetchily accepts this but asks for time to think about it. This wish is seemingly granted. However, we next see him stripped to his shorts and facing the harsh brightness of a photographer's lights as his face and form is captured on film. What is he being prepped for? He is next taken to the day room, the long hall of tables full of men quietly occupying themselves that he stumbled into during his first visit to the Company. An orderly shows him to a seat while a Company colleague dispenses medication for the assembled day room occupants who are the stoned coalface of the Company, like a corporate typing pool who require sedation to see them through the unrelenting repetition of their quotidian reality. The stranger who stared at Arthur Hamilton on that first day stares now at Tony Wilson.

'Hello Arthur – it's me, buddy. Fidelis Eternis...'

In that moment, Wilson realises that this stranger is, or perhaps more correctly *was*, his old friend and Harvard doubles partner, Charlie Evans. Like Wilson, Charlie is waiting in the day room for another second chance. It was also from this room that he telephoned Hamilton more than once in the early hours to make him his recommended Company client.

The full implication of Charlie and, possibly, all of the other day room occupants being failed Reborns doesn't entirely sink in for Wilson. He is too caught up naively thinking about where he went wrong with his first attempt at a second life and that his next attempt will work out.

'It's going to be different from now on. A new face and a name. I'll do the rest. I know it's going to be different.'

Suddenly, the surgeon who performed Wilson's cosmetic procedure enters the day room and calls for a 'Mr. Carlson'. The name is to Evans what Hamilton is to Wilson; Charlie rises from his chair in a state of emotional relief. This is clearly the start of his next stage. Wilson is pleased for his old friend.

'I have the feeling you're going to make it this time.'

He's sure that it will be his turn again soon.

It will be. That tie between Hamilton/Wilson and Evans/Carlson would seem to be very binding. In another meeting with Ruby, Wilson is insistent that he is unable to suggest somebody else as a new Company client, expressing instead his impatience for more surgery and his own next step as another somebody else. With Wilson sent back to the day room, Ruby rings Processing.

'On Wilson 722 – I think we can go to the next stage now.'

In an echo of the moments leading up to his signing of the Company contract and his first surgical procedure, Wilson is woken by the Old Man who heads up the Company. In that same sweet and folksy bedside manner, he explains a little about his founding of the Company and his own young hopes and dreams.

'I sure hoped you'd make it, find your dream come true.'

Twinkly-eyed, wistful, he confesses to Wilson that the Company has a high percentage of failures.

'Heck, we make mistakes but we admit them and go forward... You can't give up, and you can't let the mistakes jeopardise the dream.'

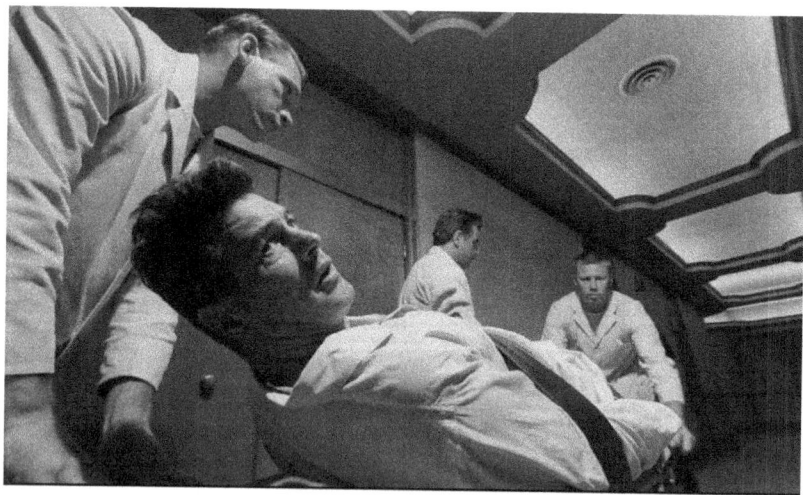

Three orderlies wheel a gurney into the room and, despite Wilson's agitation at this unexpectedly swift move to the operating theatre, he still climbs aboard the gurney upon the Old Man's request to do so. Belted to the stretcher, he is wheeled along the corridor where a man calling himself 'Dr. Morris' begins to read a passage from the Bible, except that it is cut-up quotes from different sections of the Good Book – Deuteronomy 28, Exodus 33, John 11, Isaiah 41 – a mishmash of lines appropriate for Wilson's progression to the 'next stage', and a nonsensical reference to religion that is interestingly the first and only such religious reference, given that the entire film grapples with notions of existentialism.

The horror of his coming demise dawns on Wilson and the orderlies need to restrain him further. He struggles but to no avail. The surgeon is ready for him and, as the anaesthetic takes effect, the sound of a cranial drill and the brilliance of the operating theatre lights obliterate Wilson's world. The very last thing we see is a long shot of the Malibu beach that Wilson once walked on, now occupied by another man, quite probably Evans, or Carlson, or whatever name the Company has issued to this client, enjoying the life thanks in part to the suitably identity-stripped deployment of the cadaver that was once Arthur Hamilton.

Notes

1. At the time, Saul and Elaine Bass were also working with Frankenheimer on another 1966 release from the director, the Cinerama spectacle, *Grand Prix*.
2. According to John Frankenheimer's commentary for the Criterion release of the film, this scene was shot on location at Grand Central Station in New York, not on a studio set. Many of the passers-by are neither actors nor extras but commuters going about their daily business, none the wiser when it comes to the film camera, which Howe and Frankenheimer had stuffed in a suitcase with a shooting hole in the side that they rolled along to create the low angle perspective. At times when the camera was in view, mainly involving actor Frank Campanella ('Man at Station') wearing a 'Snorricam'-like harness (see chapter SOUND | VISION for more on this), they created a diversion – a fake love scene between a male model and Playboy bunny being filmed on the Grand Central station stairs – so their own, less demonstrative shooting would go unnoticed.
3. In 1966, Frances Reid had only recently been cast on NBC's daytime soap opera *Days of our Lives* as Alice Horton, a role through which she would, somewhat ironically yet also affectionately, assume the status of America's soapie matriarch across the 40-plus years in which she played this character. *Seconds*' Emily reveals much of the stoicism and fortitude that would imbue Alice Horton.

4. "Honest Arnie": the Used Cow Dealer was an actual business – truth being stranger, and more appropriate, than fiction.
5. There is a correlation between the Company's cup of tea and the same as used to send Chris Washington (Danial Kaluuya) to 'the sunken place' in Jordan Peele's 2017 film on liberal-sanctioned racism, *Get Out*.
6. This dream sequence features one of the few custom-made sets used in this film, constructed to be physically distorted, made even more so by Howe's use of an 18mm lens on the camera.
7. John Randolph is understood to have learned to use his left hand for the role in order to match the left-handed Rock Hudson, although blooper spotters will note that he is seen filling in his newspaper crossword puzzle on his commute back to Scarsdale at the film's beginning with his customary right hand.
8. While Rock Hudson's casting in *Seconds* was widely criticised, it would be folly to think the film's makers did not see his previous 'bachelor' roles (think *Pillow Talk* [Michael Gordon, 1959]) as providing further substance to the Wilson character.
9. The Malibu beach house used in the film was, in fact, John Frankenheimer's own home at the time of *Seconds*' making. In 1991, Tom Hanks paid close to the Frankenheimers' asking price of $3.25 million for the property. The sale featured in a *Los Angeles Times* article at the time, in which the house was described thus: 'Built in 1928 but recently remodeled, the two-storey house has two bedrooms downstairs and one bedroom upstairs in about 1,800 square feet. The master bedroom has a balcony and an ocean view. Separate from the main quarters, there is a housekeeper's room and a two-bedroom guest apartment with a kitchen.'
10. On being approached to play Nora Marcus, Salome Jens told us that John Frankenheimer said: "The reason I cast you is that you have the essence of doom."

MEMORY: 'Well you see, it all began with a big red ball'

When you can't see clearly, the world's a more frightening place, pared down to a few vague signals. You watch old films and they get that feeling exactly right. All the grain starts to work in their favour, limiting how much you can really make out. They paint a muted picture of the world where any signal that cuts through the haze seizes your attention, like a lighthouse through fog. – *Fear Itself* (Charlie Lyne, 2015)

Do you remember watching *Seconds*? Maybe you caught it late one night hidden away in the terrestrial television schedules of the pre-digital 1980s and, in the vague fog and grain of tiredness and adolescence and the 4:3 flicker of the TV signal, it inveigled its way into your experience. Maybe it was at the suggestion of a friend as something that had slipped through the cracks of your viewing history but, when finally watched, soldered itself into your brain in a way that went beyond the diversionary discovery of a mere cinematic oddity.

This book is a memory of *Seconds*. It is certainly not a *remembrance*, however. Looking back to commemorate an old film as some kind of nostalgia-inducing time capsule can often rob it of its relevance to today. The memories that it generates speak as much to *now* as they do *then*, which is a testament to the film's power to remain contemporary despite the technological and surgical advances and societal developments that have taken place during the more than 50 years that it has existed, fading in and out of public consciousness, usually dependent on the whims of film distributors.

Your own memory of *Seconds* might be fragmentary, rendered so not just by your own circumstances at the moment when you saw it but also by the film's illusory nature. If it is a film you haven't seen for a while, you might reasonably feel that it was something you have at least in part imagined, dreamed maybe. This feeling may have been amplified through your observation of the 'nightmare logic' events that befall Hamilton/Wilson on his journey. They *happen* to him, his personal impulse or hand in controlling and steering the direction of events is minimal, over and above his driven response to some vague sense of mid-life dissatisfaction. Other than turning up at the appointed time and place for his first contact with the Company, subsequently signing their contract (and then only through threat of blackmail and heavy persuasion) and later fleeing Malibu, he is propelled along the stages set for their client by the Company, locked into a cross between a production line conveyor belt and a ghost train carriage.

He is a submissive passenger, carried along by a succession of vehicles; the commuter train (onto which he is virtually swept by the swell of other commuters), the family car driven by his wife, the "Honest Arnie" meat wagon, the plane bound for Los Angeles, Nora's car en route to the grape stomp party, the Company car that picks Wilson up outside the Hamilton home and takes him back from Scarsdale to New York, the gurney wheeled through to surgery at the end. He rides them all in a state of rising yet impotent agitation. Sitting watching *Seconds* can feel like being strapped into a moving vehicle, the route and destination of which is beyond your control. You only know that it's heading towards a bad place.

Seconds is always a matter of memory, for the viewer and also the central character. Given that our protagonist dies at the conclusion, we could argue the film has been constructed *entirely* from memory – a disembodied recollection of a life that may have been lived or may never have existed. Films viewed solely through the eyes of a central protagonist who then perishes – as is the case with *Seconds*, in which every scene is 'coloured' by the Hamilton/Wilson point-of-view – seemingly function as memories from the afterlife; in this case, with Hamilton/Wilson as a zombified being – walking dead, if you will – right from the opening at Grand Central Station. If we look at another example in cinema, Billy Wilder's *Sunset Boulevard* (1950) is a standout case in point, with the protagonist's eventual demise explicitly acknowledged in the opening scene through a narration that reverberates from the grave.

Which leads us to note the use of black and white stock that contributes greatly to the perception of memory, remembrance and even make-believe. Films shot in colour will liberally employ black and white to depict dream scenes or flashbacks, signifying a portion that is imagined; an imprint from the past, psyche or elsewhere. Given *Seconds* exists solely in that which is monochromatic – at a time in cinematic history when colour film stock was readily available – we can deduce that steeping the viewer in this black and white was intentional and did not come from practical or budgetary restriction. However, even if other concerns were at play, Frankenheimer and Howe have skilfully turned a limitation into an important narrative embellishment that elevates the film in a manner that could have been hindered if depicted in vivid, full colour.

Several times during the film, Hamilton/Wilson is invited to remember. Charlie presses Hamilton repeatedly during their early hours telephone conversation; the photograph of the young Hamilton with friend and adolescent tennis partner, both wearing the same kind of wristwatch:

> 'Remember, *we gave them to each other after winning the doubles at Princeton.*'

Fidelis Eternis is etched into the underside of the tennis trophy:

> '*You scratched it there, down in the locker rooms after we won the finals –* remember?'

He is told what to do at his noon rendezvous:

> 'Remember, *use the name "Wilson".*'

As his surgical scars fade, his memories are brought forth and recorded via drug-induced regression so the Company has something on which to base the life they will provide for their client. Once he is released into the world again, the expectation is that he must now forget his first life and embrace his new existence. They effectively erase Arthur Hamilton – Ruby favours a hotel room fire as the obliterating circumstances of his 'demise' – and, in proceeding to the second stage, we can assume the fine print of the Company contract is explicit about a complete avoidance of reference to the life of Hamilton.

But, if Hamilton ever read that fine print, he failed to remember it. His mind is distracted, elsewhere, from the outset. He cannot focus on the newspaper crossword during his commute back to Scarsdale, he loses the thread of his letter dictation to the bank secretary while preoccupied with the prospect of his noon engagement, he struggles to think of the parts of his first life that are worth holding on to when questioned by the Old Man. So how confident can we be that he will take a fine-tooth comb to the 'trust instruments' that the Company insists he signs? Not that Ruby and the Old Man provide him with the time and opportunity to pore over the documents – they are presented as a thick bundle of 'standard procedure' papers awaiting his signature. In the grand scheme of things, it is an act of gross administrative chicanery.

In the fugue of his mid-life crisis, Hamilton clings to scraps of information, mere marks on surfaces – the '34 Lafayette St.' piece of paper, the *Fidelis Eternis* trophy engraving, the 'standard procedure' of the Company trust instruments, the surgical blueprints used to convert him into Tony Wilson. Through these simple scribbles, scratches and sketches, he is drawn to Malibu where, as Wilson, he is left to make his own marks, through the rudimentary daubing of lines on canvases. He struggles to paint, perhaps in part due to the reality of his artistic limitations – Hamilton was a 'weekend painter' of timid watercolours – but also because this act of creation requires the artist to reflect upon and respond to his own memories and recollections. If the terms of his second life mean that he must deny the details of his first, what does he have left to draw upon for inspiration? He hasn't lived as Tony Wilson long enough to know who Tony Wilson is, and despite the artistry of the Company surgeons in creating a new physical appearance for their client, they are not able to implant new memories, less so erase old ones.

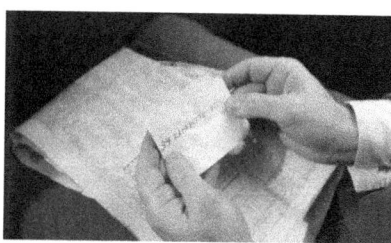 

Much like Hamilton himself, they work with scraps of his existing memory when concocting the life of Tony Wilson. The pharmaceutically derived meanderings of their client's mind that Davalo plays back to Wilson are small fragments, at best vignettes or thumbnail sketches, certainly an insubstantial foundation on which to build a new existence.

'I want a ball, a big, red one.'

His slurred, infantile mumblings at the beginning of the tape are only a little less credible than his later recorded aspirations: *'I guess I'd like to paint stuff...pictures and things.'*

And yet this is the superficial catalyst for the fabric of the life that he will live. Little wonder that Wilson is left feeling deeply insecure and susceptible to lapses in the upkeep of his Malibu façade.

As the alcohol triggers the shedding of his inhibitions during the cocktail party that he finally throws, the memory of his life as Arthur Hamilton begins to bleed through. His life as Tony Wilson is founded on regression memories, the recording and reception of which form an early event in that life, so it is perhaps not surprising that he remembers his session with Davalo during his drunken conviviality:

'Well, you see, it all began with a big, red ball'.

Through his boozy haze, he knows that he has transgressed – the 'oops' fingertips that he presses to his lips when mentioning his daughter give that away – but the price of his transgression is high. In a flash of sudden and shocking realisation, he comes to understand, not only are the men surrounding him also Reborns, they, unlike him, are engaged successfully in the public suppression of their first life memories. Wilson's undoing is that he *doesn't* forget. His surgery changes his surface but his mind remains the same. He recalls, and, as a result, like a defective product on sale in the supermarket, he is recalled.

But he doesn't go straight back to the Company headquarters. Instead, he heads for his old Scarsdale home to meet his widow, Emily. This is not an altruistic or redemptive visit; he can never come clean to Emily about the step he took in any hope that she will understand and take him back. He is literally a different man now, after all. Instead, it is an inadequate attempt to discover more about himself, at least his Arthur Hamilton self.

What he finds, however, is another near-erasure of the man he once was. Aside from the single, framed portrait photograph on the mantelpiece of the calmly anonymous living room in which Emily receives him, he is ostensibly absent. It is the exact same photograph used in the obituary column of the newspaper announcing Hamilton's demise. We see this immediately after the Hamilton-to-Wilson surgery as proof that the Company has delivered on its contractual obligation to confect the circumstances of Hamilton's death. As a lone relic of the face of Arthur Hamilton in his former domestic location, it reduces his legacy to the scale of a small ad. He probes Emily for her recollections of her husband:

> 'He was a quiet man. The thing I most remember him for were his silences.'

Perhaps Hamilton was always absent, even when he was present. At any rate, her memory of him is practically a non-memory, a silent void. Wilson isn't even offered a glimpse of the spaces in the house that he once filled; he/we do not see inside the study that was decorated with mementos of Hamilton's fishing and tennis exploits where he spoke with Charlie over the phone at the beginning. We also learn that Emily has not kept the collection of his paintings that he thought were stowed in the garage. The one memento that he takes away from the visit is the *Fidelis Eternis* tennis trophy, passed on to him by Emily like a remnant from a yard sale. Arthur Hamilton is gone.

Wilson's memory fails him back at the Company headquarters. When Ruby presses him for the name of a former colleague or associate from his time as Hamilton who he can recommend as a new client, he is unable to think of anyone from his past who is suitable. Just as his recall at the cocktail party lands him in trouble, his *lack* of recall at this point, whether genuine or deliberately evasive in an attempt to deny the Company what it wants, does not serve him well. As part of his preparation for 'the next stage', his bedside visit from the Old Man includes one last invitation to engage his memory:

'Remember, *son. We've got to keep plugging away at the dream. The mistakes teach us how. It wasn't wasted*. Remember *that*.'

Hamilton/Wilson turned out to be a mistake. He won't be wasted. Remember that.

The focus on memory and remembrance are also vital ingredients in the prevailing atmosphere of the film. We are either stuck as a fellow traveller alongside Hamilton/Wilson on the journey he doesn't choose but to which he is subjected, or trying to reclaim or simply understand an unsatisfactory past. Regardless, *Seconds* is a film that never sits 'in the moment'. Its refusal to come to a standstill creates a persistent uneasiness across the viewing experience, which may account in some way for the film's failure at the box office upon its release. It is an 'unsettling' watch, both literally and figuratively, which some find uncomfortable and unappealing.

Frankenheimer was no stranger to stoking discomfort in his audiences. The first entrant in his 'Paranoia' trilogy', *The Manchurian Candidate*, told the story of an American soldier brainwashed during the Korean War returning home as a sleeper operative poised to kill without remorse or memory on the command of his communist puppet masters. Released twelve months before President Kennedy's assassination, the film is a disturbingly prophetic depiction of Cold War politics, as it leads towards its climax in which our unwitting murderer is deployed at a political convention to 'shoot the presidential nominee through the head'.

Compared to *Seven Days in May*, the second of Frankenheimer's 'Paranoia trilogy', *The Manchurian Candidate* – also based on a novel, this time by Richard Condon – is closer to *Seconds*, especially in its thematic renderings of a lost generation of privileged white men, and how memory – or lack thereof – is used as an instrument to control, subvert and, ultimately, destroy. It is through memory, through its erasure or refusal to be erased, that the fates of these films' main characters are determined.

For *The Manchurian Candidate*'s central character of Raymond Shaw (Lawrence Harvey), being bestowed with the US military's highest award for valour, the Congressional Medal of Honor, is no recompense for his suffering as a result of war or at the hands of a heartless, ambitious mother (Angela Lansbury). In fact, when asked directly how he feels, Shaw says '*like Captain Idiot*' despite being welcomed back to

America as a hero. Shaw, the son of an influential family, has gained the hallmarks of success, yet he has been afforded this success through the fortuity of birth. Like Hamilton in *Seconds*, his accomplishments may have been partially achieved through blood, sweat and tears, yet the opportunities – to go to university, to get a prestigious job, to court a desirable partner, to make proper money rather than scrape a living – have come to him through happenstance. The dour conclusions of both films ask a broader question of what success actually looks like.

Dr. Yen Lo (Khigh Diegh, who reprises his smiling assassin persona from *The Manchurian Candidate* in *Seconds* as Davalo) justifies the brainwashing of Raymond Shaw – or 'conditioning' as he prefers to call it – in the following way:

'Without memory of his deed, he cannot possibly feel guilt... Having been relieved of those uniquely American symptoms – guilt and fear – he cannot possibly give himself away.'

However, Shaw is never fully conditioned; neither are his army buddies who routinely wake from their sleep with night sweats and recurring nightmares. Their subliminal recollections all hark back to a ladies' garden club meeting in a hotel lobby in New Jersey. These soldiers wait languorously and draw back on cigarettes, distractedly looking into the air, while gussied-up older women discuss the intricacies of growing hydrangeas. In reality they are in Manchuria, China, where their captors are describing a revolutionary new brainwashing technique to other communist masterminds, a technique to which each one of these US soldiers has been subjected.

Shaw is a closed book, although detailed with extreme psychological anguish through a tightly drawn performance from Lawrence Harvey (another gay man in reality, like Rock Hudson). The other soldiers, mainly personified by Major Marco (Frank Sinatra), give us a clearer insight into the reality of the 'brainwashee'. With memories that can no longer be relied upon, they exist in a confused state. They may not remember their capture but they can remember the minutiae of every day, such as Marco's rote recall of Eugénie's (Janet Leigh) apartment number. Marco even voices his confusion at his conditioned response to praising Shaw as *'the kindest, bravest, warmest, most wonderful human being I have met in my whole entire life'*, while, in actuality, he considers Shaw to be a cold and prickly character.

Similar to *Seconds*, there is little surprise *The Manchurian Candidate* does not end well. Much of this positing can be attributed to David Amram's score that includes a melancholic 14-note statement over the title credits, executed on trumpet (not coincidentally, reminiscent of a military bugle and the Commonwealth's use of *The Last Post* at ceremonial events such as commemorations and funerals) that immediately evokes a reflective tone; that this film will always be looking backwards rather than forwards.

Hamilton's memories cannot be erased; instead, he is meant to ignore them and conjure new ones as Wilson. Shaw may not be able to remember his Korean experiences but, just as Hamilton struggles to ease into his new life because of the memories from a former one, Shaw grapples with the suppressed recollections that are bubbling under the thin veil of his consciousness. He might not be able to recall, but to recall is to know that he is an assassin, which offers him no escape from his mental torture. In effect, though, both men are unwilling to let go of that which makes them who they are – their memories – and it is this that seals their fate.

As John Frankenheimer said in his commentary on *Seconds*:

> *'One of the reasons this movie means a lot to me is that it says something I firmly believe: that in life, you are the result of your experiences – the result of your past – your past makes you what you are today. If you take away your past, you don't exist as a person.'*

ARTIST | SURGEON: 'You were my best work'

Only a few kinds of images force you to shut your eyes: death, suffering, the opening of the body, some aspects of pornography for some people, and for others, giving birth. In this case, the eyes become black holes in which the image is absorbed willingly or unwillingly, these images are swallowed up and hit just where it hurts, without passing through the usual filters. – ORLAN [Mireille Suzanne Francette Porte], reproduced in D. Pastourmatzi (2002) Biotechnological and medical themes in science fiction

Seconds aspired. It wanted to be a work of art emerging from the everyday world, projected onto screens like impressive photorealistic graffiti applied to the walls of buildings. The repeated use of distortion is a conscious attempt to pull the image as it appears on the flat surface of a screen into a state of startling three-dimensionality.

There are moments in the film, especially the entire opening credits, that are reminiscent of anamorphic artwork. The creation of images stretched beyond recognition that only appear recognisable when viewed from a particular angle is a technique that dates back to the days of da Vinci ('Leonardo's Eye' from 1485) and Holbein the Younger (the diagonally elongated skull to be found in 'The Ambassadors' from 1533) and persisted through the *trompe l'oeil* of Baroque murals, the curios of Victorian children's parlour games and the odd 1970s progressive rock album cover (see the sleeve design for Rick Wakeman's 1976 release, *No Earthly Connection*).

Anamorphosis literally deceives the eye; it is a trick, an optical illusion. For many, it is a stilted exercise in clever draughtsmanship and is, therefore, less art and more contrived novelty. *Seconds* has, at times, been received not as art but as *arty*, dubbed so derogatorily. Frankenheimer clearly strove for a European art cinema aesthetic, arguably too keenly and deliberately. The film is eager, anxious even, to show that it is in revolt against the Classical Hollywood paradigm but it is so, perhaps, only superficially. It presses hard for ambiguity, partially resolved narrative, visual flourish, directorial expressivity, an emphasis on location filming, hand-held camerawork, conspicuous breaking of the '180-degree rule' and all manner of other editorial and cinematographic rule-breaks. To some, though, the art is skin deep, an artificial assemblage of constituent parts that fail to pass as the genuine article. It's no small irony that this criticism is so close to serving as a basic description of the *Seconds* story, and is also its strength.

When discussing the style of painting their client might consider adopting in his new vocation as a painter, Davalo the guidance advisor, embodying the Company, offers a summary list of suggested artistic approaches during Wilson's post-operative analysis: '*Surreal, primitive, impressionistic, whatever*'.

It displays an unsophisticated appreciation of art. It doesn't really matter to Davalo or the Company which technique Wilson prefers; they can provide him with a start-up body of work painted by somebody else and arrange it in the studio of the Malibu beach house as part of the general set-up and simulacra of their latest Reborn's new situation. Wilson's works of arts are forgeries of course, just like the diplomas and certificates of study from reputable universities the Company provides to legitimise Wilson's artistic reputation. Davalo insists these documents are bona fide and valid but the entire business of the Company is founded on forging the identity of its clients, making the world believe their tragic death has occurred and passing them off as somebody else. These forgeries also serve to mirror the phoniness of Wilson's first life as Hamilton; the signifiers of success that he has worked so hard to achieve reduced to rubble, merely counterfeit mementoes. The artifice presented by the Company is everything that defined his middle/upper-class existence. All his achievements now mean nothing, if they ever meant something, because they are so easily duplicated, passed off as 'the real thing', just like his life – hubris with no value.

The walls of the office in which Hamilton first meets Ruby and the Old Man before signing the Company contract are decorated with paintings. We glimpse Picasso's 'Mother and Child' from 1921 among them – copies, naturally. Another mother/child painting, artist unknown, can be seen facing the Picasso. Both are images intended, no doubt, to suggest the implicit parental nurturing tendencies of the Company – except that the latter canvas, viewed at a distance, is somewhat more reminiscent of Goya's 'Saturn Devouring His Son'; that horribly cannibalistic image representative of the conflict between youth and old age. Behind the large desk in the office hangs a large work of abstract expressionism. We only see it briefly before Ruby pulls down the blank projection screen directly in front of it onto which the blackmail film of Hamilton ravaging the Company female is shown. Chaos masked by a manipulated version of events.

In his first life, Arthur Hamilton's watercolours are absent, unseen. They don't even survive being stored away out of sight in the garage. His Scarsdale home doesn't appear to be decorated with them. Instead, we catch sight of a print of 'The Music Lesson', Vermeer's painting from 1665, on the wall of Hamilton's study when he takes the telephone call from Charlie in the early hours. It's an image that is mirrored by the room in which it hangs. Much like the painting, there is a single light source (Hamilton's desk lamp) and a ceiling of strong horizontal shapes. The *Fidelis Eternis* tennis trophy on the mantelpiece to the right is even an echo of the pale white jug on the table on the right side of the Vermeer painting. A mirror hangs on the wall in the room in the painting, much as the print hangs on the wall of Hamilton's study, creating the basis for a *mise en abyme* – an image within an image. The scene represents an entry point for Hamilton; the phone call is the catalyst, and the room-within-a-room visual presentation establishes him on the brink of a downward-spiralling continuum. Given the point in the film when this painting appears, the Vermeer print can be read as a subtle portal and likened to the rabbit-hole in *Alice's Adventures in Wonderland*, with Charlie Evans as the white rabbit that Hamilton follows. At the bottom of the rabbit-hole, we'll soon see Hamilton experience the effects of a drugged 'DRINK ME' cup of tea.

The Company makes no secret of its pride in Hamilton's rebirth as Tony Wilson. Post-surgery, the Old Man calls him 'a masterpiece' and then, when the experiment fails, the surgeon laments the loss of his 'best work'. Upon arriving in Malibu, Wilson is encouraged to throw a cocktail party as a way to introduce himself to the neighbours, which is pitched to Wilson as an opportunity to settle into his new persona, although one can't help suspecting this is also the Company wishing to show off, to parade Wilson as their latest and greatest 'stud bull' – or 'masterpiece', if you wish. Wilson is reticent to play host and, when he finally succumbs to the pressure, ends up making quite the exhibition of himself, not the kind of exhibition the Company was hoping for.

Unless the Company possesses a separate facility that we are never privy to, it would appear that their client base is exclusively male. The female presence on the premises extends to the nurse who greets Hamilton upon arrival and directs him to his drugged cup of tea and the recumbent woman who Hamilton subsequently ravages under the influence. Otherwise all staff, surgical team and supplicants waiting in the Day Room are men.

Far from denigrating women, Frankenheimer and his screenwriter Carlino have effectively absolved women of responsibility in the *Seconds* universe. They are couched as employees; if not, they are witnesses, those on the outside looking in, or – let's be honest – glorified prostitutes (employees of another sort), which is essentially the role Nora plays when she is contracted to seduce Wilson and ingratiate him into his new life. This is a film about what men do to themselves and each other. It is careful not to make gender statements, without taking women out of the picture altogether, but it does so in a mid-20th century manner, which means some critics may be tempted to see it in terms of today's gender politics, which simply don't exist in this film.

In the form of the 'Old Man', played by Will Geer, we are provided with a founding father figure, a good old boy, a kind of Colonel Sanders of the Kentucky Fried Chicken empire. Older than Hamilton – conceivably old enough to be his father, sporting a straw boater, walking cane and a Mississippi drawl – he materialises in the Company office to ease Hamilton into completing the documentation once Mr Ruby's cheerful officialdom has failed to capture a signature. His role is a handholding one, delivering the 'now, now, everything will be alright' reassurance that any man would require, even the suicidal kind, when signing their life away.

Despite its commercial and critical failure, *Seconds* arguably triggered a loose and short-lived cycle of Hollywood films concerned with the loss of purpose and direction seemingly being experienced by white, middle-class, middle-aged males in America – from Frank Perry's *The Swimmer* (1968) to John Cassavetes' *Husbands* (1970) – although such a cycle had already been foreshadowed in American literature, from John Updike's *Rabbit, Run* (1960) to Richard Yates' *Revolutionary Road* (1962). In the late 1960s and early 1970s, the middle-aged man in America was lost. He looked back on his life and suddenly realised all of the things that he had been taught were important and meaningful (family, career, social status, right and wrong, trust in the establishment, etc.) left him with a yawning chasm of emptiness. Accordingly, Hollywood of the 1960s attempted to depict these middle-aged crises and their protagonists' searches for meaning. Often in these journeys, the middle-aged man would meet the antidote to his troubles in the form of a member of the counterculture, often in the guise of a young, nubile hippie girl, who would temporarily open his eyes to a more meaningful existence. Ultimately, most of these films neither spoke to Middle American audiences or to the youth market but were spectacular (in every sense of the word) failures; fascinating in their mixed messages and values. It is in this purgatory that *Seconds* also lives.

Matthew Weiner's television series, *Mad Men* (2007-2015), used the clarity afforded by hindsight to examine this white, American, male crisis, with the beginning and end of the '60s loosely acting as the show's bookends. In the character of Don Draper (Jon Hamm), and across seven seasons, this series methodically unpicks the intricacies of such existential angst in considerable detail. Draper – a handsome, highly successful advertising exec; the-man-who-appears-to-have-it-all – functions as the embodiment of this male cultural breakdown, grappling to reconcile himself with his identity and desperately burying his pain with women and booze. In a mid-series twist that brings the show into closer alignment with *Seconds*, we discover the identity Don Draper is wrangling with isn't even his own: he has taken the name of a fellow soldier in the Korean War. However, as *Seconds* had already taught us, assuming the identity of someone else doesn't mean escaping yourself; hence his downfall. Created almost 40 years after the fact, *Mad Men* proved an easier pill to swallow for audiences and critics than the films tackling the same subject matter contemporaneously. Where such themes cut too close to the bone in the 1960s and even the '70s, *Mad Men*'s creators had the luxury of temporal distance, which resulted in their series being a giant success.

By his own admission, Frankenheimer did not intend for *Seconds* to be a wilfully non-commercial picture. By definition it could hardly have been classified at the time as an 'arthouse film'; it was a major studio production featuring one of the biggest stars of the day. In an interview, though, the director confessed, given the audience reception of Rock Hudson in the role of Wilson, his casting decision had been a bad call, despite the commitment Hudson brought to the role:

> 'He worked his ass off, and I think he did a good job. But strangely enough, and I'm quite serious, the movie was ruined commercially when I cast him. People who would go to see *Seconds* would not go because Rock Hudson was in it, and people who would go to see a Rock Hudson movie would not go to see a movie like *Seconds*.' (Eagle & Frankenheimer 1977)

The fact that the film was submitted for competition at the 1966 Cannes Film Festival suggests it was not universally abhorred; there were those who recognised *Seconds* for its brilliance, and its boldness to go where no film had gone before. However, much to Frankenheimer's disappointment, the Cannes screening was greeted by boos from the audience. Only when its adored star stood up in the crowd did those jeers turn into thunderous applause, but in truth they were applauding Hudson for his body of work and not the film they had just watched.

Aged 35 at the time of making *Seconds*, Frankenheimer was still too far shy of middle age to identify with the character of Arthur Hamilton but his similarities to the 'younger' Wilson cannot be ignored. In casting the dark and handsome Hudson in the role, he was somewhat casting in his own image, the notoriously egomaniacal Frankenheimer sporting a brand of magnetic good looks that would have made him just as comfortable in front of the lens. Agent Arthur Axelman wrote of him:

> 'His looks were important, because, like the most popular kid in school, he was always the best-looking man in the room and on any set. It was reported when he directed Rock Hudson in *Seconds* that Frankenheimer was the better looking of the two. He was indeed movie star handsome, even well into his sixties. He also had enjoyed a reputation as a lothario, with an open marriage and a multitude of affairs with his leading ladies.' (Axelman 2011)

The idealised life 'styled' for Wilson reflects that which Frankenheimer was actually living, in both its perceived utopia and the perceived liberties it offered a trapped man, as well as the sordid realities that lurked beneath such a façade. With a string of hits under his belt, including the two other films of the 'Paranoia trilogy',

Frankenheimer was one of Hollywood's leading filmmakers; the world being his metaphorical oyster, and yet, as a political liberal jaded by the American system, he would descend into alcoholism and eventually take respite from his filmmaking in France where he underwent cooking tuition at the famed Cordon Bleu institute.[1]

Those who admire Frankenheimer would have no issue labelling him an artist, although his approach to artistry was not one of an auteur. He learnt his craft flying-by-the-seat-of-his-directorial-pants in the less than arty realms of live television drama; the TV industry then being the red-headed step-child to the movie industry, despite proving a fertile breeding ground for an exciting, new guard of American filmmaker – Frankenheimer, Sidney Lumet and Arthur Penn, to name a few.

Auteurs are largely defined as those filmmakers with so much influence over their works they are thought of as their authors, even though filmmaking is a collective creative pursuit that has many 'authors'. Accordingly, auteurs usually function as both the writers and directors of their own artwork (i.e. their films).

Frankenheimer was not a writer, and never assumed that role.[2] Unlike many other directors, he routinely invited his writers on set and would often defer to them to honour their intentions. As an artist – and his career output certainly positions him as one – Frankenheimer was fundamentally a highly accomplished technician who could masterfully slot together the various moving components that somehow combined as a motion picture. He was something of a surgeon; slicing, dicing, assembling a team of other similarly highly accomplished practitioners who could bring his vision, and that of his screenwriter, to life.

By the mid-1960s, there was a new breed of actor emerging – complicated anti-heroes, embodied by the likes of Warren Beatty, Paul Newman and Robert Redford. Rock Hudson was under contract with Universal but was feeling frustrated due to his pigeonholing into fluffy matinee idol roles that weren't moving with the times. Films such as *Pillow Talk* (Michael Gordon, 1959), *Man's Favorite Sport* (Howard Hawks, 1964) and various Sirkian melodramas had made his career but, despite their excellence, were struggling to sustain it. He sacked his long-time agent Henry Wilson, the coincidentally surnamed man who had crafted the 'Rock Hudson' persona from country boy Roy Fitzgerald, ended the relationship with Universal and hired a new agent, John Foreman. It was Foreman who then met Frankenheimer at a party and convinced him to consider Hudson for the lead in *Seconds*, as unlikely as that pairing may have sounded. But Frankenheimer (2013) eventually saw what Foreman was getting at:

> 'If you look at it, he was a kind of invented personality, wasn't he? He identified with this guy; the fact that, if you destroy your past, then you're nothing – you can't function. And, to become Rock Hudson, really, he had to destroy a great deal of his past.'

In writing his authorised biography, 'Rock Hudson: His Story', Sara Davidson says of the star:

> 'There is no Rock Hudson. There are many Rock Hudsons. He projects what will appeal to the person he's with, and he will get that person's heart at any cost.'

> 'Trying to understand Rock Hudson was like trying to penetrate a sphinx. The more I looked, the more mysterious and disturbing the details of his life become. Every day there was a surprise, a new contradiction to resolve, and before long, there was nowhere I could put a foot on firm ground. It was like treading on a spider's web.'

> 'I found that nothing could be taken at face value. Even if Rock had told the same fact to ten people, it might not have been true. He loved secrets and seemed to enjoy throwing people on a false scent.' (Hudson/Davidson 2007: 15)

If the casting of Rock Hudson in *Seconds* may seem incongruous, Davidson's insight says the opposite: this was the role he was born to play. A man created by an industry (i.e. Hollywood), given a new identity (i.e. Rock Hudson) and shackled with a fraudulent existence to support it (i.e. ladies' heartthrob) flew in the face of everything he represented, whatever that was. No one really knew him. In light of this, it's little surprise that Salome Jens, playing Nora Marcus, reflects on her experiences working with Hudson in *Seconds* in the following way:

> 'He was an actor's actor. He was not a movie star – he was a star. And he was good. He was always willing, open and able. So, no matter what, knowing that he was gay or whatever, I fell in love with him. Absolutely. As far as I was concerned,

he was a man – totally a man – and I was in a man's arms.' (Interview with co-author)

If *Seconds* is John Frankenheimer's masterpiece, then Rock Hudson is the muse by which that masterpiece was made possible. The symbiosis of star and creator – the Frankenheimer/Frankenstein analogy – runs deep through the making of *Seconds*.

Wilson's Malibu home was the current residence of John Frankenheimer at the time of shooting the film and, by all accounts, was furnished exactly as the Frankenheimers had furnished it, with very little art direction. The paintings on the walls are modern in style, typically representative of the mid-20th century, the inference being they are the works of Tony Wilson; however, it is sometimes difficult to tell where Wilson ends and Frankenheimer's influence begins. Note the drugged Hamilton/Wilson's first career choice of professional tennis player – Frankenheimer was reportedly so skilled at tennis (Baxter 2002) he considered turning pro (and, indeed, continued to play tennis across his entire life). Yet, instead of tennis, Frankenheimer opted to be an 'artist'; maybe not a visual artist like Wilson but an artist, nonetheless, in the form of a filmmaker.

Even within the stylised visual contortions of *Seconds*, there is a sense of the non-fiction, most pronounced in Frankenheimer's eschewing of staged sets, preferring on-location filming as much as possible. For example, rear projection was still liberally employed for car scenes in the 1960s but Frankenheimer and Howe went to great lengths to rig up cumbersome car mounts to shoot the driving scenes in *Seconds*. Similarly, accepted practices of substituting 'day for night' were replaced with real dusk, dawn and night shots. Frankenheimer's apprenticeship in live TV drama no doubt went a long way in influencing this approach. Almost in spite of its consciously arty exterior – *surreal, primitive, impressionistic, whatever* – *Seconds* is a reflection of its era, as indicated through two men representative of all of a certain social standing. It is a document, a documentary, a State of the Nation, and a work of art.

The surgery in *Seconds* – that transforms the sagging, lagging Arthur Hamilton into the vital, virile Tony Wilson – is the mid-way turning point of the film. It is the fulcrum upon which the narrative sits and from which the performative baton is passed from John Randolph to Rock Hudson. It is also the 'creation scene' of the film;

the moment the Company unveils its 'Da Vinci', although it's a self-congratulatory moment because their achievement cannot be announced to the world. Not only is this scene pivotal from a thematic stance but, from a technical perspective, the filmmakers' talents were being tested; they needed to successfully sell Randolph's transformation into Hudson in a segue that stands up to both conceptual and visual scrutiny. While the premise of turning one man physically into another has its origins in classic storytelling (think *Dr Jekyll and Mr Hyde*), that which is deemed impossible still needs a modicum of believability if it is to hold sway with an audience. If Frankenheimer et al. had failed to pull it off, the second half of *Seconds* would have been utterly redundant.

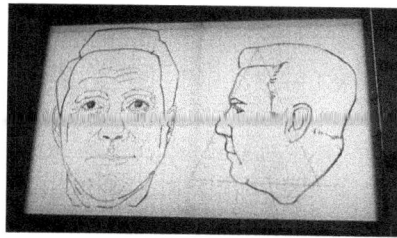 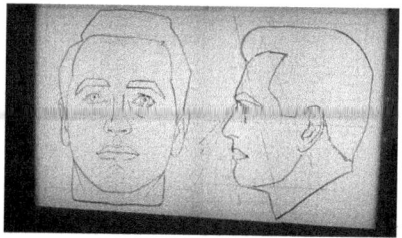

Frankenheimer (2013) readily conceded that creating the transition from Hamilton to Wilson was his hardest task in making the film:

> "I can't emphasise how much care we took to try make the transition from John Randolph to Rock, to make it believable.... To have Rock Hudson look badly at this time of his life was one of the great achievements in cinema. Nobody was better looking than Rock Hudson.'

However, Salome Jens argues the concept of such physical transformation was not as far-fetched at the time as one may initially think:

> 'I did a one-woman show of Marlene Dietrich, and Marlene knew exactly what to do to enhance her beauty and to remain young for the movies. That was something that's a Hollywood art. That's part of it. So that didn't seem strange to us at all and certainly not unbelievable at all [when making *Seconds*], except the fact that the organisation would create your death and the whole thing; that was what was mysterious and fascinating.' (Interview with co-author)

Additionally, in 1966, the first sexual reassignment clinic was opened at Johns Hopkins Hospital in Maryland by a team of progressive doctors. Although this clinic was opened surreptitiously with no fanfare, due to the controversial nature of their objective, its inception still demonstrates that great leaps in surgery were being made by the mid-1960s, which helped give credence to the *Seconds* narrative.

Before *Seconds*, an iconoclastic French film, *Eyes Without a Face* (Georges Franju, 1960), paid intimate attention to the ins and outs of cosmetic surgery to sell the arguably outlandish premise that someone could physically take the face of another. While *Eyes Without a Face* is culturally and sub-textually different to *Seconds*, they both embody a 'Frankenstein complex' together with the fallacy that taking someone at 'face value' is a noble acceptance of truth. In *Eyes Without a Face*, Alida Valli's character – the Ygor to Frankenstein – even says to the doctor, "*I've known you long enough to read your face*", which is symptomatic of her naivety rather than any familiarity with the person in question.

Similarly, another film released in the same year as *Seconds*, Hiroshi Teshigahara's spectacular Japanese sci-fi gem, *The Face of Another*, overtly addresses the idea of masks affecting the wearers and even changing their personalities. The surgeon, more excited about his accomplishment than his patient, says, '*Once you get used to the mask, you'll be a new man... one with no records, no past. A mind invisible to the world*' to which the protagonist then exclaims with frustration '*I'm me!*'. He even visits his wife wearing his new mask to test whether she can recognise him. The parallels to *Seconds* are obvious.

Some may consider the long surgical scene in *Eyes Without a Face* as gratuitous, but it is largely through this clinical dissection of the procedure – a labouring on the intensity of the surgery, the protraction of cinematic time to give it a 'real-time' sense – that the central concept of the film is sold. Without it, the idea that this genius doctor could rebuild his daughter's disfigured face would feel so flimsy and far-fetched that we, the audience, would be emotionally divested. Sometimes, it is too easy for critics to dismiss that which could be deemed 'graphic' in cinema when it actually serves a very important function.

Likewise, *The Face of Another* takes a long-winded approach to selling its surgery. In laying the rubbery mould over burnt skin, the surgeon and his nurse apply a thick cream over his entire face, which, according to the film's exposition, is intended to blend the mask more seamlessly into its wearer. But this narrative device serves another purpose: of helping the audience make the visual jump from pre to post-op.

The dialogue-free surgery scene of *Seconds* contains footage from an actual rhinoplasty procedure, which produces queasily graphic results.[3] No doubt as a means to get up-close and personal to the surgery, the footage is hand-held with a more pronounced grain than other scenes in the film, which helps emphasise the realism, not to mention the roughness at which the surgeon handles his patient, standing in stark contrast to any theatrically produced depictions of surgery.

There are constant edits between the kidney bowls and surgical tools of the procedure and crude before/after diagrams upon which the surgeon (played by Richard Anderson)[4] and his medical team are basing their reconstruction. Given the non-specificity of these drawings, they serve as a clever means to join the dots between Hamilton and Wilson, aiding the viewer in taking that mental leap of one man mutating into the other, while remaining the same man.

Wilson emerges from surgery in a mummified state. By doing so, the filmmakers are still bridging the divide between Hamilton and Wilson – and milking the suspense – keeping him swathed in bandages. Above the slits for eyes, nose and mouth, we can see unruly grey hair, as he is yet to fully become our new-born Adonis. The surgeon takes the time to delve into the minutiae of his artistry and explain to us (and him) how '*everything is different*' – from his teeth being ripped out and replaced, and a complete vocal cord resection to the removal of his fingerprints. He has squared off bones and tightened ligatures, and now Wilson will have to undergo several months of physical conditioning, which is depicted in a short montage without labouring the point.

As the viewer of *Seconds*, you may ask yourself why anyone would agree to such surgery without having approval over the outcome. This is a question the filmed version of the storyline neglects to tackle; however, David Ely's novel provides a more than satisfactory explanation. When negotiating his contract, Hamilton/Wilson asks,

'Look here... don't I get a change to, um, approve the... final version beforehand?' To which he is then told: 'Well, we used to do that, but we found that our clients could never really come to a decision. They kept adding a little here and waiting to take a wrinkle out there, and really, it was a terrible nuisance, and so we dropped that feature.' (Ely 1963: 45) Which all seems very viable corporate rationale for such a decision.

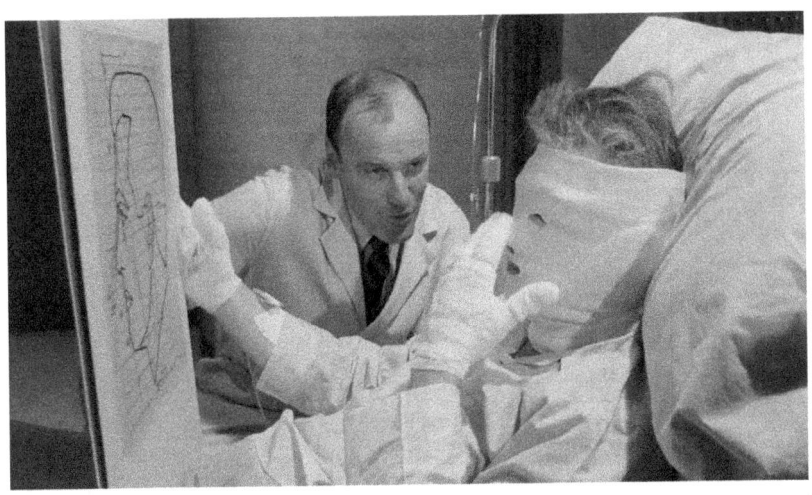

In the film, the combination of visual and spoken exposition goes a long way in helping us believe it is indeed possible that John Randolph could become Rock Hudson. The original intention was to have one actor play both sides of the Hamilton/Wilson character. However, once Rock Hudson was chosen for the role, he insisted that he only play Wilson. It's now hard to imagine it coming together any other way.

The writer Armistead Maupin makes an illuminating observation of Rock Hudson:

> Not long after I met Rock, I noticed he had this deformity on his thumbnail; a really deep groove that ran down the middle of the thumbnail. I observed that Rock was in the habit of taking his forefinger and rubbing it against his thumbnail as a nervous tick, a repeated thing he did over and over and over again, and he'd deformed his thumbnail in the process. I later thought of that as the perfect little

symbol for the closet; the notion that this secret you have to carry finds its way out in some way until it actually deforms you. (Maupin in 'Rock Hudson: Acting the Part', Biography [1999])

One could say that the PR 'surgery' undertaken to manipulate Roy Fitzgerald into the Rock Hudson image eventually revealed its cracks; the pressure of who Fitzgerald/Hudson *really* was pushing its way to the surface, even in the subtlest of ways: the constant worrying that would eventually deform his thumbnail. In most respects, Rock Hudson was far more successful than Tony Wilson. He maintained the façade for decades, while just one night on the booze was all it took for Wilson to crack.

Artist and surgeon: two pursuits that are occupied with the deconstruction and reconstruction of matter into something wonderful. As a technician, Frankenheimer worked with surgical precision but, within the broader science of his craft, he showed an intense appreciation for the artistic. In the year previous to *Seconds*, he made the World War Two action drama *The Train*,[5] a film that contains dialogue in its finale about art that feels somewhat poignant considering the negative reception accorded to *Seconds* upon its release. When Paul Scofield as a Nazi colonel confronts Burt Lancaster's railway man, who has successfully thwarted the colonel's attempts to smuggle a trainload of French national art treasures back to Germany, he remarks:

'A painting means as much to you as a string of pearls to an ape... The paintings are mine and always will be. Beauty belongs to the man who can appreciate it. They will always belong to me or a man like me.'

Perhaps a similar sense of rarefied exclusivity put paid to *Seconds*' box office performance. Away from avowedly arthouse cinema hits, popular audiences don't tend to take too kindly to films that pitch themselves as works of art best suited for the attention of the privileged few. The unorthodox aesthetic trappings of the film may have proved too rich for many peoples' blood, but metaphorically speaking, by declining to unpack the painting from its protective wrapping, by refusing to remove the bandages from the face, both critics and public alike failed at the time to witness a film that encapsulated so much of their sociocultural predicament. All we can do is appreciate it now and hope to make up for lost time.

Notes

1. John Frankenheimer died in 2002 at the age of 72 from a stroke, a direct consequence of complications following spinal surgery.
2. In his audio commentary for the Criterion DVD release of *Seconds*, Frankenheimer talks about how beneficial he found it to have the writer with him as much as possible. Frankenheimer says Montgomery Clift told him "we both like working on dirty paper – after someone else writes it, we know what to do with it."
3. Six crew members fainted during the shooting of these surgeries so Frankenheimer himself stepped in to help James Wong Howe capture the footage.
4. As well as being a regular in Stanley Kubrick films, Richard Anderson would famously appear as the boss of two other genetically modified fictional characters – Steve Austin (*The Six Million Dollar Man*) and Jaime Sommers (*The Bionic Woman*).
5. Frankenheimer took over the directorial reins of *The Train* after Arthur Penn was fired by Burt Lancaster.

SKIN | MEAT | FLUID: 'Sure you don't want this chicken?'

But time strips our illusions of their hue,
And one by one in turn, some grand mistake
Casts off its bright skin yearly like the snake.
– JUAN, & BYRON, G. G. B. (1822). *Don Juan. Cantos III. IV and V.*

Seconds consumes, digests and expels. As viewers of the film, we are devoured at the very beginning, fed into the mouth of the bandaged head in the opening credits, and we are essentially carried through the story 'within' the singular experience of Arthur Hamilton/Tony Wilson. We perceive regular images from Hamilton/Wilson's field of vision – albeit skewed at times, a mirroring of his contorted state of mind – and we undergo the stages of the process through which he passes, like mute travelling companions, aware that he/we are being led beyond our control along and down a path that will not end in a good place. At no point does *Seconds* allow us to feel at ease or believe this Hamilton/Wilson situation will end well.

The abattoir through which Hamilton is taken on his convoluted route to the Company should give the game away – he is a piece of meat entering a production process that will render and package his very substance. We, having entered his system at the outset, make our own way through him/the film. As we digest the film, it digests us. Even in David Ely's source novel, there is a line where Wilson is told, '*They handed you all that crap about love and rebirth, and now you find out it's just a butcher shop, just like everything else.*' (Ely 1963:)

Throughout the numerous stages of the process, Hamilton/Wilson keeps encountering doors that close behind him, cutting off any possibility of returning to his dull but safer, more predictable past life. The commuter train door slams, separating him from the Company messenger who recedes back into the throng on the platform as the train departs. The doors of the "Honest Arnie" van are fastened with Hamilton inside, transported in the back like a side of mutton to the Company headquarters. The doors of the elevator slide shut behind him when he enters the headquarters but there are no call buttons on the corridor wall beside this point of entrance – this is a one-way journey. Whenever he seeks to retreat or retrace his steps, Company officials promptly curb him, the Pepto Bismol to his reflux.

Manipulation of skin is part of the Company's business. If we consider the very walls of the corridor to be within their organic realm of control, we might conclude that, having facilitated Hamilton's entry into the organism, the 'skin' of the walls has seen fit to exercise its capabilities and 'heal' itself. The elevator call buttons are subsumed, the doors sealed, Hamilton has been successfully delivered and then effectively injected 'under the skin' of the Company.

Hamilton himself closes the doors of Ruby's office at the beginning of their first meeting, a meeting that will end with his no-going-back signing of the Company contract. When Wilson backtracks to Scarsdale in the third act, he stands briefly on the threshold of the front door of his former family home greeted by Emily's maid. Our view of him, from inside the house, is screened by the gauze of a storm door. Although he is invited in, that initial semi-transparent visual divide suggests the house itself has grown fresh skin over the wound of his death.

The final set of doors that Wilson passes through are those leading to the Company operating theatre, where his descent through the system will end. It's a dirty business but disposal of its waste is an integral part of how the Company operates. Consumed, digested, expelled, Hamilton/Wilson is ultimately little more than food passing through the 'doorways' of a system; chopped up, chewed up, washed up.

Aside from the Saul Bass credits, *Seconds* shares with *Psycho* a narrative trajectory that can be likened to the human digestive system. Consider the post-credits opening sequence of the Hitchcock film; an aerial shot of the city of Phoenix that enters the mouth-like window of a hotel room and comes to rest on the sandwiches by the bedside of the lovers, Marion Crane (Janet Leigh) and Sam Loomis (John Gavin), during their illicit lunchtime tryst. The symbolic mastication of this first love scene serves to break open and extract the film's starter exposition – the couple's passionate desire to be together constrained by their lack of money – which is chewed up and washed down ('hot as *fresh milk*') in the following scene set in Marion's place of work, the real estate agent office managed by her boss George Lowery (Vaughn Taylor) when she 'swallows' the $40,000 in cash entrusted to her to put in the bank by Lowery's profligate client, Tom Cassidy (Frank Albertson).

Marion and the money begin their journey down the alimentary canal highway between Phoenix and Fairvale – Sam's hometown – before arriving in the 'stomach' of the film, the Bates Motel. More sandwiches are washed down with milk provided by Norman Bates (Anthony Perkins), this time in Norman's office parlour, before the knife of 'Mother' and the digestive juices of the shower prepare Marion for the final part of her journey, down the plug hole and through the intestinal tract. The third act passage of characters around the stairwell and corridor bends and angles of the Bates house amount to the colonic processing of waste, leading ultimately to the nasty rectal discharge below stairs in the form of Mrs Bates. The death-doll husk of Norman's mother is a foul embodiment of fecal rot, a last deathly excretion that plays semi-subliminally across Norman's face as he squats in his police cell before the dissolve to the concluding sewage trap that is the swamp where Marion's body was dumped.

Much like the Phoenix hotel room open window 'mouth' in *Psycho*, our entry into *Seconds* is through the gaping, quivering mouth of the bandaged head at the end of the opening credits, and right away we are travelling though the oesophageal passage; the inside of the 'mouth' of Grand Central Terminal, the epiglottis and alimentary canal of the commuter train line to Scarsdale, the digestive stages of the steam presses at the dry cleaners and the carcass hooks at the "Honest Arnie" abattoir that Hamilton passes through, the 'stomach' chamber of the Company rooms and corridors. The knife of the Company surgeon carves into Hamilton and prepares Wilson for his dispatch to Malibu, where he tumbles into the digestive juices of the macerating wine press and stumbles through the flowing drinks of the cocktail party before embarking upon the inevitable journey down the intestinal tract, from Scarsdale back to the Company and his final expulsion courtesy of the 'Cadaver Procurement Section'.

At the very end, we share his final point of view on the operating table. Accompanied by the sound of the cranial drill crunching through his skull, we experience the white elimination of the surgical lamp prior to death and the expulsion of his processed corpse. Not unlike *Psycho*'s ultimate lavatorial swamp, the very final shot of the ocean suggests a flushing away of the resulting dead body, like so much effluence.

Symptomatic, perhaps symbolic, of his dissatisfaction with the life that he has, Arthur Hamilton seems to suffer from recurring indigestion. Stress, anxiety and depression are all contributors to digestive complaints, and our hang-dog Hamilton has weathered more than his fair share of such ailments, no doubt hammering them down deep into the corners of his subconscious, given it was deemed unbecoming for a man of that era to openly admit to any mental 'weakness'.

When cross-examined by his wife, Emily, he irritably refers to 'just Old Faithful' as the source of his ill feeling when returning to bed after his late night telephone call, suggesting that it is a chronic digestive problem and, with it, resolutely silencing her from further questioning. His noon appointment at 34 Lafayette Street is preceded by more dyspeptic distraction at the bank when dictating a letter to his secretary. Indeed, he appears to skip lunch in order to make it to his appointment on time.

He moves among the unappetising frozen cowhides strung up at "Honest Arnie" and, on arrival at the Company headquarters, is offered symbols of civility: a cup of tea and a sandwich. Perhaps he would have eaten the sandwich, but a drink of the drugged tea means he fails to get a bite. When he regains consciousness and meets Mr Ruby, a plate of chicken arrives, although Hamilton declines to eat it this time, wary no doubt after having been drugged once, which leaves it for Ruby to pick over enthusiastically in one of the film's more comic (relief) moments.[1] The greasy-fingered gusto with which Ruby devours the chicken, processing yet another carcass, demonstrates that, by comparison to their client-to-be, the Company has a sharp appetite.

'Sure you don't want this chicken?'

Hamilton keeps declining. Shortly after surgery, Wilson is informed that his surgeons have performed a complete vocal cord resection on him, and that all of his teeth have been extracted and replaced with a new permanent set. With it, they've taken his voice. No one will listen to Wilson; or, at the very least, Hamilton has definitely been rendered permanently mute because he no longer exists. It will take Wilson a while before he can talk again, and no doubt eat properly too.

During the early stages of his Malibu residency, we see Wilson sitting at a table twice, first outside on the terrace and then inside in the dining room. John is fussing with plates, knives, forks but there is no food to be seen, nothing to suggest that Wilson has enjoyed a meal, or eaten anything at all for that matter. He is poured an aperitif cocktail and an after-dinner coffee. He drinks neither. The only thing that he is seen to put into his mouth between leaving New York and meeting Nora Marcus on the beach are some stress pills in the plane restroom intended to quell his panic attack. Even these pills are shown to be knocked back, washed down and uncomfortably swallowed.

It seems like the stranglehold of inhibition continues to affect his peristalsis until Nora's influence frees him up. When they first meet on the beach, she runs into the tide with flower child abandon but Wilson isn't ready to get his feet wet. Feeling more relaxed as the encounter progresses, he drains the cup of tea that she makes for him back at her beach house, enabling her to read his tea leaves and thereby begin to unlock the man.

They were clearly caught in bad weather because Wilson's hair is wet. Nora, stroking his damp locks, muses: '*The good things always happen with the rain.*'

Large raindrops strike the porch outside behind her. With the rain, with the imbibing of the fluid, his passage is eased – rehydration improving digestion. His ability to successfully break down and absorb that which he has consumed then meets a challenge in the form of the Santa Barbara grape stomp party. He wants Nora to introduce him to new experiences but, by accompanying her to this hedonistic event, has he bitten off more than he can chew?

Flesh is exposed, fluid is freed – the grapes give up their juice under the combined weight and tread of the revellers and, despite his initial reluctance, Wilson is eventually broken down and succumbs to the baptismal fluid of the wine press. The knot of restraint in his stomach is released, the obstacle is removed. This, it seems, is what he wanted, and what he was promised by the Company: freedom.

Yet, this newfound relaxation leads to further reflux and regurgitation at the subsequent cocktail party. With the free flowing alcoholic beverages, he freely exchanges saliva with Nora in a string of passionate kisses, and to further illustrate the leakage that his newfound freedom is causing, he first deliberately pours a cocktail onto the carpet to demonstrate his ability to control his drinking, then later accidentally spills a drink over one of his guests.

His leakage continues. As the party chat flows, *mein host* lets slip some memories from his first life. Even in his soaked state, he tries to stem this loosened tide of utterances, first with a full hand clapped to his mouth, then with guilty 'excuse me' fingertips pressed to his lips. Out of Wilson's mouth comes the gas of Hamilton's past, acid memories that he is expected to suppress. His bought-and-paid-for freedom relies on the suppression of any urge to regurgitate the details of his former life, so when his tongue is loosened by liquor the other Reborns at the party are forced to step in.

In an effort to claw his way back up and out of the system that has swallowed him, Wilson returns to the Hamilton home but finds barely a trace of his old self there. His old study has been completely redecorated, even his watercolours have been removed from the garage and disposed of. Emily has effectively washed her hands of her husband. He is collected and returned to the Company headquarters, adamant that he should be allowed a shot at a *second* second life, with another new face and identity. But the requirements cannot be met, and with his inability to sponsor another client triggering 'the next stage', Wilson is prepped for his final evacuation, as the trussed up and tethered corpse-to-be, destined to be utilised as a suitably disfigured and unidentifiable cadaver of convenience, shat out the other end. The cranial drill that penetrates his skull and ends his life can be heard crunching through bone and entering the soft tissue of his brain. Reducing solid to liquid, life floods out and away, the Californian tide ebbs and flows, and the beneficiary of the Hamilton/Wilson cadaver gets to walk along the shoreline. And so the cyclical Company digestive system continues.

To corrupt a popular phrase, Hamilton is quite clearly uncomfortable in his own skin. The aging process, perhaps a few too many bank executive lunches and the sedentary nature of the commuter lifestyle, has led to middle age spread and the baggy flesh of his jowls combined with his permanently weary, drawn expression lend his face the characteristics of a loose-fitting mask. Usually, the ravages of age are presented as the burdens of women; consider the likes of Gloria Swanson proclaiming 'Alright, Mr De Mille, I'm ready for my close-up' or any of the other *Grande Dames* of Hollywood's Golden Age who, by the 1960s, had embraced 'Hagsploitation' as a means to recycle their careers.[2] But, in its Faustian way, *Seconds* plays to the vanity of mankind with Randolph's Hamilton willing to 'do a deal with the devil' for just one more go at it.

The miserable flesh mask that Hamilton wears is most graphically emphasised when Emily attempts physical intimacy to take his mind off the worries he is reticent to discuss. His mask is impenetrable, even with what should be the warm, loving kisses of a wife. Her kisses are met with lips that entirely fail to muster a matching pucker. In his anxious disconnection, Hamilton stares past her, through her – a thousand-mile stare – without a flicker of reciprocation. The skin, the mask, hangs; chin doubled under the crude pressing of lip against lip. The eyes glaze over, his sexual appetite having long since waned. His mid-life situation has numbed him to the physical experience. Even before Emily's sexual advance, the couple is depicted wearing head-to-toe nightwear in a room that contains two single beds, rather than the usual marital double, framed in such a manner that draws the eye to the heavy, parallel beams overhead. Such geometry gives weight to the situation – the Hamiltons have something heavy hanging over their heads – which is consequently reflected in their sagging faces and general world-weariness.

James Wong Howe's camera captures 'the kiss' in a series of handheld shots; extremely close, intrusive even, and unflatteringly exposed with harsh, hard lighting. Even Frances Reid, as Emily, unlike other actresses of the time, is not spared the severity of such unkind lighting, no Hollywood 'beauty' lensing to soften her or her male lead. We are so close that we can see the hair in Hamilton's ears and, when Emily's advance meets its fateful death and Hamilton sinks back into his pillow staring upwards at the beams overhead, beads of sweat stand out on the surface of his skin. In fact, Hamilton sweats a lot, which acts as his nervous 'tell' or tic – his version of worrying at his nails – betraying that which is repressed.

When under the influence of the Company's drugged tea, Hamilton is demonstrably compliant and malleable when filmed in the act of molestation – upon viewing the resulting reel of film, Ruby confesses *'of course, the drug made it easier to manipulate you into the proper positions and attitudes'* – but, apart from having his strings pulled for the purposes of the Company cameras, his demeanour is the same as that seen in his bedroom at home; the blank, expressionless face, the unblinking gaze of sexual disengagement. It is as though Hamilton's outer layer has become little more than an impassive, plasticised fat suit.

Contrast Hamilton's dispassionate pre-operative liaisons with Wilson's eventual post-operative carnal skirmishes with Nora during the cocktail party; his kisses are positively carnivorous in their fervour (*'You're beautiful…you're an ocean!'*).

Wilson at this point is a wellspring of emotion, and in this state he practically eats Nora's face. His phrasing closely echoes that of Nora herself during their first meeting by the sea when she runs impulsively into the lapping tide: *'Ocean, I love you! You're beautiful!'* As he assaults her face with passionate kisses, he simultaneously takes the words right out of her mouth.

Despite the blank and lifeless discomfort that it displays, Hamilton's skin is porous and does exude fluid, although the beads of sweat that repeatedly prick his brow and upper lip – on the commuter train, in bed after his telephone conversation with

Charlie Evans, as his succumbs to the drugged tea – seem like a symptom of the struggle for restraint and the stress of upholding respectable decency in a socially uncomfortable situation.

Wilson breaks significant sweat twice; first as a consequence of the inhibition-loosening cocktail party catharsis, which ends with him pinned to his bed by the other Reborns who are trying to shut him up, and then as a result of his inability to sponsor another Company client and the literal restraint he experiences when belted onto the gurney for delivery to the operating theatre at the end of his life. The effort of his struggle *en route* to surgery in these final minutes leads to a veritable deluge of perspiration, the moisture emanating from his face distributing haphazardly through the repeated thrashing of his head.

Pressed down, frantic and screaming, we see Wilson's face soaked and contorted with motion blur, completing a sub-ellipse that began with a very similar image at his point of release among the grape-treaders. That starting point was one born of hedonistic release but not unlike the ring of Reborns forcibly constraining him in his Malibu bedroom and the Company orderlies strapping him onto the gurney and plugging his mouth with a sponge. However intense this moment of wild abandon appears with the strangers in the grape-treading barrel, is he really any more liberated rubbing juice-slicked shoulders with these people than when he was among the milling hordes of commuters at Grand Central Terminal? However wildly alive he feels once he is naked and revelling among the flower children, is he really any more alive than the row upon row of dead bovines swinging from their hooks at "Honest Arnie"?

Of course, only when it is too late does Wilson begin to fully realise any of this; that what the Company has given him is merely a repeat of the first life that he had, albeit one dressed in the trappings of apparent freedom, choice and self-determination. When deposited in the Day Room upon his return to Company headquarters, and left to wonder how long his enforced limbo will last, he absent-mindedly nibbles at a tiny rasher of crispy bacon. With his thoughts so occupied, his earlier mistrust of Company food seems forgotten. As last suppers go it is meagre, but also appropriate; Wilson is reduced to simultaneously eating and being an ultimately insignificant piece of processed meat.

Indeed, like some dystopian ouroboros, he has reached the point in his Company-determined life cycle when he is practically and symbolically consuming a piece of himself. Swallowing his tail, he is locked inside a nightmare mash-up of the rabbit-hole in Alice and an inescapable 'Möbius strip' continuum. He enters to the taste of the 'drink me' drugged cup of tea, he prepares for 'the next stage' with this 'eat me' scrap of meat.

> *'The years I've spent, trying to get all the things I was told were important, that I was supposed to want. Things. Not people or meaning. Just things. And California was the same. They made the same decisions for me all over again, and they were the same things, really. It's going to be different from now on. A new face and a name. I'll do the rest. I know it's going to be different.'*

Watching Wilson closely, fellow Day Room resident Evans/Carlson, having washed down some pills handed to him by an orderly with a little cup of water from a tray, now weeps out that water as Wilson ruminates over his recent past and pictures his future. As the direct beneficiary of Wilson's actual fate, Evans'/Carlson's tears are the liquid by-product of relief and a form of selfish gratitude, not exactly sorrow at the thought of what he knows awaits his friend.

Not unlike the various fluids produced by Hamilton/Wilson – his perspiration at different stages, his semen (we presume) during the staged ravaging of the Company female – the tears of Evans/Carlson are practically squeezed out, excreted under pressure despite his best efforts to keep them in. For a man to cry in the very male-oriented setting of the Company, he risks a leaked admission of comparative feminine weakness. Wilson himself wept when he first saw his new face in the mirror, upon the removal of his bandages after surgery. It's a human reaction, a little reflex dam burst of the man's emotions, something that we can't imagine the previously pent-up Hamilton doing. For all its natural flow, however, the Company might have judged Wilson's tears to be a sign of his inability to keep his feelings hidden.

Hamilton has a foretaste of Company machismo when he is led through the "Honest Arnie" refrigerated interior. The abattoir foreman who takes him through bellows insult-strewn instructions at his all-male workforce.

> 'Let's go, you bunch of idiots. Get that beef cut down. Damn! Get that truck going and get the meat the hell out of here! What are you gonna do, take all day? Don't let those hooks fall off! Let's move it. Come on! Let's hook it off! Hook off! Don't just stand there. Move that beef off the line! Let's go! What are you, a bunch of jerks? Come on! Go! Go!'

The masculinity of the meat handlers is a marked contrast to the relative reserve of the banking world in which Hamilton is familiar, and to which he has modulated his limbic responses. There is no polite restraint here within this place of hyper-masculinity. The foreman treats him with comparative gentility as he packs him into the back of the meat wagon for delivery to the Company headquarters. But this 'kid gloves' handling doesn't diminish Hamilton's obvious discomfort at being in such an aggressively male environment.

Later, when Ruby seeks to gain Hamilton's signature on the contract, the soon-to-be client baulks at the meal that is brought before him, giving Ruby permission to pick over the remains. Hamilton literally can't handle it. Ruby's desire to eat Hamilton's dinner is expressed initially with an innocuous enough question:

> 'Sure you don't want this chicken?'

The simple introduction of a comma into the sentence subtly changes the tone of the words and converts them into a sly impugning of his masculinity:

'Sure you don't want this, chicken?'

To not eat the meat, to not sign the contract, would be tantamount to male ineffectuality, further emphasised in Hamilton's experience of impotence with his wife. It is while picking through the bones of the meal that Ruby ruminates over the circumstances of the 'death' that the Company will concoct for Hamilton.

'The victim of some kind of machinery, an explosion. A hunting misadventure.'

He raises these relatively dramatic prospects almost to highlight how unsuitable they would be for a man who he considers to be mundane. Wiping the grease from the chicken off his fingers with a napkin, he then suggests:

'I had thought perhaps a hotel room fire.'

A comparatively banal ending but one that will render his corpse anonymous and provide a suitable pause for the Company to then go about resurrecting him as a Reborn. Once the procedure has been performed, a mummified Hamilton-Wilson is told by his proud plastic surgeon:

'I expect you to be prancing around here like a stud bull.'

It is another recall to the meat-market processing into which Hamilton/Wilson has been admitted. Yet now, the 'carcass' of Hamilton is some other 'man to the slaughter' who has failed to meet his obligations as a Reborn, with Tony Wilson poised to emerge from the chrysalis of his post-surgical wrappings. He does so with new dentures and new fingerprints, and some Frankenstein-esque suture markings to the face, wearing an expression that indicates nothing beyond the tenuously oppressed emotional responses that defined Arthur Hamilton.

Tony Wilson is the scar tissue that holds Arthur Hamilton within. And scar tissue is weak; a fragile epidermis that could break at any moment, which is the brittle stasis in which Hamilton/Wilson now exists. His wounds may heal, disappear from visibility, but Hamilton is never far below the surface. The months of rehabilitation and 'conditioning' that the Company subjects him to, do nothing but make a trimmer, more outwardly appealing man out of Arthur Hamilton. His surgeon may boast that *'everything is different'* but this 'everything' is only skin-deep.

As a middle-aged actor returning from the confinement of the 'Black List' after approximately 15 years, in playing Hamilton, John Randolph was rushing to make up lost time, countering the opportunity to play youthful roles that were denied him. *Seconds* was the perfect vehicle for this actor released from professional limbo, giving him the means to express the frustration of those missing years in a role that could also, hopefully, facilitate his reinvention as a Reborn actor.[3]

In the real-world mirroring make-believe, the 'Company' is Paramount Pictures, which is ironically (or not) the way Rock Hudson refers to the production in a short promo video that was recorded during the making of the film.[4] More than a few of those who have worked in Hollywood, either in front of or behind the camera, could possibly relate to such an analogy. But none more so than Hudson, a complete construct of the Hollywood machine that moulded him, gave him a new name, taught him to act in an image that flew directly in the face of his real self.

As far as *Seconds* goes, there was no more cathartic an expression than the Hamilton/Wilson portrayal from its dual male leads; two men who had been digested and spat out by a filmmaking machinery with the sole mission to make money, regardless of any altruistic façade it might otherwise project. Everything in Hollywood is only skin-deep; *Seconds* had the gumption to tell it like it is.

Notes

1. According to Frankenheimer's Criterion release audio commentary, the idea of the chicken was not scripted but came out of rehearsals with the actors.
2. The Hagsploitation phenomenon (or 'Grand Dame Guignol' or even 'Psycho-Biddy') was seen as a vehicle for formerly glamorous actresses to revive their careers in leading roles by portraying monstrously unbalanced 'hags'. Notable films in this sub-genre include *What's the Matter with Helen?* with Shelley Winters and Debbie Reynolds, *What Ever Happened to Aunt Alice?* with Geraldine Page and Ruth Gordon, *What Ever Happened to Baby Jane?* with Bette Davis and Joan Crawford, and the formerly mentioned *Sunset Boulevard* starring Gloria Swanson, among many other titles.

3. John Randolph was far more successful than Arthur Hamilton. This second wind in his career would be prolific, with roles in the likes *Escape from the Planet of the Apes* (Don Taylor, 1971), *Conquest of the Planet of the Apes* (J. Lee Thompson, 1972), *Serpico* (Sidney Lumet, 1973), *Earthquake* (Mark Robson, 1974) and *King Kong* (John Guillermin, 1976), among many other television and big screen titles until his death in 2004.
4. This 'making of' clip can be found on YouTube (https://youtu.be/1OzjQAQJ6Zc) and includes Hudson describing the film thus:

   'Well the film I'm working on now is called *Seconds*. It's certainly a different type of picture and certainly a different role for me. It's almost a horror movie, certainly a suspenseful movie and certainly very dramatic.'

SEX | DRUGS | ROCK | PAPER | SCISSORS: 'There's a kind of gathering...It's going to be very wild'

Now see here, Jekyll! Dash it all, as your most trusted colleague and friend, I beg you, before it's too late, to give up these diabolical experiments! Think, man! You are going *beyond*. You are delving into things that no man, not even a physician, has a right to know. Remember, Jekyll, the horrible happenings of 1920, when poor John Barrymore attempted these experiments. And again in 1932, when Frederic March did the same thing. And Spencer Tracy in 1941! I tell you it's monstrous what you're doing! No, no, Jekyll! Pour out that smoldering liquid! Don't drink it! Stop! STOP! Now you've gone and done it. Well, take another sip and change back, or millions and millions of Rock's fans will never forgive you. (Taken from 'Topsy-turvy flashbacks to yesteryear's films', a photo article in the December 20, 1963 edition of *Life* magazine)

Seconds both transgressed and regressed. Its protagonist passed from hidebound to hedonistic by way of severe social and physical discomfort at a point in history of great and rapid socio-cultural upheaval. But his attempts to loop back and play out another different future left him fatally ensnared in the marginal space between the two worlds. The narrow interiority of the Company headquarters acts like the oblique stroke between before/after. It divides and separates yet binds the two together, a connecting corridor that for Arthur Hamilton/Tony Wilson promises to be a route out of mid-life mediocrity but proves to be a trap that ends in clinical mutilation, a thin, skewed purgatorial slash-cum-corporate abattoir. The means by which the Company embroils its clients is a disinfected variation of the Oldest Profession. It is essentially a colossal, elaborate escort enterprise, promising physical, emotional and – by extension – sexual freedom and pleasure yet, ultimately, delivering torment and treating the customer as commodity, pound for pound. The corporate costumes merge: executive suits, surgical scrubs, butchers' aprons. The business premises loop and interlace; slaughterhouse, beach house, charnel house. Company clients are always usable body parts, from start to finish; weighed, measured, processed.

In Hamilton's case – and why should we doubt that it would be different in any other?

– sex is used to both entrap and entice. The Company female who Hamilton is filmed ravaging is deployed to ensure that he signs the contract. The prospect of revived sexual pleasures as part of Wilson's 'freedom' manifests in Malibu in the form of Nora Marcus who, of course, is no less of a Company employee than the female Hamilton was filmed molesting back at headquarters. Promiscuity comes at a price: $30,000 and the eventual requisitioning of the client's physical properties in the service of the business. Hamilton/Wilson passes between realms of pleasure and pain, typically either pushed or pulled through by the forces that control him. He is both consumer and commodity, a mode of exploitation often considered the lot of females in the mid-19th to mid-20th century specularised culture of modernity. Applied to mid-1960s Hamilton/Wilson, the role of purchaser/purchased is a distilled commentary on postwar western malehood – breadwinner as sliced bread.

The Company offer is tailored to appeal to men of a certain age, emasculated by their circumstances, told to want more, aware of the cultural wellspring of change defined by free love that was beginning to fulminate around them, yet too old to feel like a natural participant in that change. And this 'change' in America in the 1960s was not inconsequential.[1] Traditionally dominant and conservative Christian values – bear in mind, America even branded its legal currency with the words 'In God we trust' – were being publicly challenged, with the year of *Seconds*' release, the numerically diabolical 1966, proving one of the most pivotal. Specifically, on Good Friday – a date that implicitly signifies change within a Christian belief system – *Time* magazine published its infamous 'Is God Dead?' cover image and feature, which the editor, John T. Elson, felt captured the rise of 'the new atheism' (as he coined it) and America's general shifting mood in theology.

Religion was undergoing radicalism, and its adaptation to this New World following the upheavals of the first half of the 20th century was being debated on all fronts. One such text was Richard L. Rubenstein's response to the Holocaust, *After Auschwitz* (1966), which questioned pre-conceived notions of a Judeo-Christian God, in light of the atrocities committed during the Second World War. Along with the hypothetical death of God, America was still mourning the loss of its own god-like figure with the assassination of President John F. Kennedy in 1963. Women were taking control over their reproductive health – and men were simultaneously losing control over women – with the introduction of the contraceptive pill and the rise of feminism.[2] Timothy Leary was calling for people to 'tune in, turn on and drop out' with the aid of hallucinogenic drugs, which ushered in a whole new form of existential angst. Pop and movie stars were emerging as the false prophets, with John Lennon even proclaiming The Beatles' popularity among contemporary youth as being greater than Jesus.[3]

Out of the ashes of this dramatic dismantling of 1950s conservatism rose 'The Black Pope', Anton La Vey, who grew up in California, an area he deemed to be the epicentre of the 'darkest manifestations of the American Dream' (and where Wilson would be relocated by the Company). On 30th April, 1966 – exactly 30 days after *Time*'s 'Is God Dead?' cover outraged the nation – La Vey formalised the Church of Satan and, with it, a symbolic antithesis to the old America. Despite its provocative name, La Vey's Church of Satan does *not* believe in Satan as a spiritual being that actually exists, nor does it believe in Christian or Islamic constructs of the Devil. The Church of Satan is atheist in principle, using the representation of The Devil as an archetype of pride, individualism and enlightenment; all very real human traits – natural, God-given human traits, one might say – that La Vey claimed were suppressed by other religions. Anton La Vey defined Satanists as those who are 'outsiders by nature, living as they see fit'. It is, therefore, hardly surprising that his brand of Satanism would appeal abundantly to the unbridled egotism of Hollywood types, with the likes of Jayne Mansfield, Sammy Davis Jr., Liberace and Kenneth Anger all famously answering his call. He was also enamoured of cinema, his genre of choice being German Expressionist films, including Fritz Lang's *M* (1931) and early *Dr. Mabuse* adaptations (1922 and 1933) and Robert Wiene's *The Cabinet of Dr Caligari* (1920).

Stylistically, *Seconds* is not far removed from German Expressionism. Its black and white palette, stark geometry and contorted camera lensing are hallmarks that defined the Expressionist movement, along with elements of film noir. *Seconds* also eschews any overt references to God or religion – except for the halfhearted ramblings of Dr Morris in the film's finale that are, in their bastardising of religious mantras, a coarse rebuke of religion, whatever religion that may be. Even the older woman at Wilson's 'coming out' party, when commenting *'there is such a religious climate out here, don't you agree?'*, is referring to her more pagan-like proclivities for routinely changing sects – '*virgin sacrifice and all*'.[4]

One might argue *Seconds* takes an atheist stance in its exploration of one man's existentialism, and that the most religious moment of the film is salaciously channelled through a kind of sexual liberation – the Bacchic grape stomp – a very carnal moment in which Wilson finds himself unwittingly initiated into a rapturous group of 'outsiders by nature, living as they see fit'. As Hamilton/Wilson, he resists participating in this fevered orgy of pleasure; a 'bankerish soul' as David Ely described him in the original novel, holding onto the conservatism of his awkwardly erased past. But then the headiness of the counterculture breaks down his reserves, and he succumbs to that which is inevitable; a new, reactionary dawn. Anton La Vey would, undoubtedly, approve.

The grape stomp scene is unique to *Seconds* as a film; it was not included in the original Ely book. The filmmakers recognised the need for a central rite-of-passage to signify Wilson's rebirth – but how to do that proved a major sticking point until producer Edward Lewis mentioned a 'wine festival' in Santa Barbara; a ritualistic, annual event run by a bunch of hippie intellectuals.[5] While this scene features nudity and oodles of wild abandon – and vine leaf crowns, goblets and small musical instruments – it does not feature sexual activity beyond kissing. However, through its emotional explosiveness and the transformative euphoria that literally erupts from the film's protagonist, this is a 'sex scene' in the figurative definition of the term, and it's more sexual than any transactional sex that takes place prior to this moment. In the 'climax' of this scene, Wilson even cries out 'Yes! Yes! Yes!' over and over again, which is possibly the most utilised exclamation at the point of sexual climax aside from 'Oh God! Oh God! Oh God!', the choice of less biblical language being far more appropriate here.[6]

Sean Easton, in his essay on the classical motifs running throughout *Seconds*, makes much ado of the ritualistic nature of this Bacchic scene, its depiction of an actual festival, and its ties to classicism (including the incorporation of the character Nora Marcus, and the classical resonance of her surname). It is a long scene, and Frankenheimer goes to great lengths to faithfully honour the mini narrative that is played out as part of the ritual, as Easton outlines:

> 'First comes a procession to the festival place. When they arrive at the site of celebration, the processional leader, who wears around his neck a leopard skin (a token of Dionysus), invokes various deities (59:38–59:45), including Pan and "...the gods of this place".'

> 'A participant, having been declared Queen of the Wine, strips, climbs into the vat, and begins stomping the grapes, followed by the leader and numerous celebrants. The rest gather around, dancing and drinking. Two separate shots of the area around the vat reveal a statue modeled broadly after the archaic Greek style (1:01:59) – in the second shot it is adorned with flowers (1:03:41). The identity of the statue for the revellers is not specified, but it likely represents for them either Dionysus himself or at least the ancient Hellenic pedigree of the festival.'

> 'When the vat is packed with the naked bodies of men and women of various ages, a drunk, ecstatic Nora Marcus approaches the distinctly uncomfortable Hamilton/Wilson, exhorting him in Dionysian terms to yield to the wildness and freedom of the moment (1:03:50–1:04:39).' (Easton 2012: 205-206)

The dialogue for the scene matches up thus:

> Nora: '*Now the season ends, and the old vines are buried deep. Now, in dying, Bacchus gives us his blood... so we may be born again...* [laughing] *Come dance with me.*'

> Wilson: '*Nora, I don't know any of these people. I don't think...*'

> Nora: '*Don't think me, Tony! Don't! I came here to feel – to be! I'm dying –and that's the world* [gesturing toward the vat filled with revellers] *– the whole bloody world!*'

> Wilson: '*It's not a question of dancing. I'm not part of this!*'

> Nora: '*I'm dying – and that's the world – the whole bloody world!*' [turns toward vat, stripping off her clothes]

> Wilson: '*Don't! Nora! Nora! Hey, Nora!*'

According to Frankenheimer's DVD commentary, the look of fear we see on Rock Hudson's face is not acting, it is real. Salome Jens echoes this confession saying she too initially questioned their intrusion on this hallowed ritual.[7] Yet, somehow, the heightened emotional energy of the refusal and then submission on behalf of the actors is what gives the scene its impact and makes it so unique, affecting and irreplicable.

As the frenzy of the grape stomp grows, so does the cutting of the film. With the removal of clothes, we see a loose repetition of shots, mainly that of women unbuttoning their brassieres, although captured from behind so, while the scene may reveal glimpses of nudity, it never ventures into the gratuitous. The short-duration shots edited from handheld cameras create a swirling sense of motion and emotion, with elation being the dominant mood that ruptures through the surface. It is stylistically removed from any other scene in the film. These ritualistic revellers wear expressions of ecstasy, and they join in the festivities without restraint, demonstrating full trust and complicity.

Then there is Wilson, who has been an outsider/onlooker at every point in his journey so far, walking through his own storyline in a state of near sedation, who is now forced to cross that line and become a full participant in the headiness that unfolds around him; that which the Company has profiled as being consistent with the personality of Tony Wilson.

'Stomp those grapes! Stomp those grapes!'

As Arthur Hamilton, Wilson may have been permitted to disappear or blend into the background at social events but, as Tony Wilson – the handsome, debonair bachelor – he cannot fade into the scenery so easily. Instead, everyone wants a piece of him, to be part of the fun, so they can mingle with and partake of his physical attractiveness. Ironically, as Wilson, Hamilton is no longer able to be himself.

If Nora had chosen not to jump into the vat of grapes, maybe, just maybe, Wilson could have got away with not participating. However, as soon as Nora starts her monologue and breaks free from Wilson to also tear off her garb and jump in the vat, his fate is somewhat sealed. Yet again.

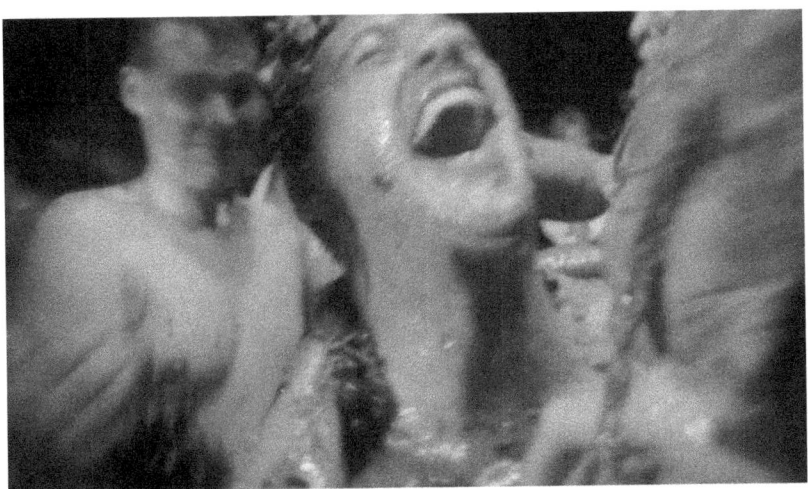

With Nora in the vat, he is unhinged, untethered. The strangers around him converge and, wilfully oblivious to his ardent protests and obvious distress, drag Wilson kicking and screaming towards the vat before tipping him in head first. In a different context the scene could easily appear to be some kind of bizarre gang rape, as they rip off his clothes and claw at his body with glee. Like the drugged molestation at the Company office, this is another sexualised interaction that occurs without Hamilton/Wilson's explicit consent. It also goes a long way to illustrate how, despite the promises of liberation, Wilson has little control over the writing of his new story.

There is a point, while clutching onto Nora with tonnes of pulverised grapes and their juices flying around them, that Hudson as Wilson flicks the emotional switch from distress to euphoria. It is *the* moment of climax, perfectly acted and timed from Hudson – the '*Yes! Yes! Yes!*' moment – a moment that easily trumps the double-take he performs when his bandages are removed and he sees himself transformed into Wilson for the first time.

'*Maybe that's part of turning the key,*' Wilson had said when asking Nora in her Mustang if he could accompany her to this wild gathering in Santa Barbara. It is in this scene that the key is turned. Within a narrative of almost endemic gloom, this is the scene where Wilson is, figuratively, touched by God and, covered with grape residue representing afterbirth, he is indeed Reborn. Maybe there is a chance of happiness for Wilson? We are afforded just a sliver of hope but, if the scene's correlations to gang rape indicate anything, this is nothing more than false hope, and the filmmakers snatch it away from us immediately.

Following a short segue by the sea where Nora and Tony repose in intimate embrace, the next major scene is the cocktail 'coming out' party intended to cement Wilson's place within the community. By comparison to the grape stomp, it is a decidedly sober affair (not withstanding Wilson's insistence on getting drunk), populated by buttoned-up, suited male guests accompanied by their wives. It is also where, despite his grape stomp breakthrough, any hope for Wilson well and truly dies.

Experiencing *Seconds* can frequently be anything but pleasurable. Occasionally, it is positively unpleasant, a perfectly legitimate feeling for a film to engender if the makers' goal is the deliberate discomforting of the audience as a means of delivering a provocative message. Much of the unpleasantness comes from the often-overwhelming sense of manipulation of Hamilton/Wilson that we are led to feel and share. In every respect he is controlled – think of him as a 'controlled substance' – and those controlling him resort on more than one occasion to the administering of a sedative or other such narcotic or mind-altering chemical substance.

It's a repeated pattern of sedation and control that finds form in the stylistic and technical choices of the filmmakers. The disorientation and paranoia that is achieved through lens choice, editing and shot set-up selection, let alone theme, can leave the viewer feeling drugged, less as a result of any self-administered recreational opiate – this is the antithesis to the counterculture psychedelia of later films such as *The Trip* (Roger Corman 1967) and *Head* (Bob Rafelson 1968) – than due to the covert administering of a medication intended to render one suggestive and compliant.

Hamilton finds himself under the influence of one or other kind of sedative four times while in the hands of the Company. He is given a spiked cup of tea upon arrival at the Company's office, which enables them to stage and film his ravaging of the girl. His post-operative psychiatric regression in the care of the Company's 'guidance advisor' Davalo is induced through the administering of pentothal and caffeine sodium benzoate; a 'truth serum' cocktail that recalls the post-war western fixation with mind control and brainwashing in the 1950s in general, and the themes of Frankenheimer's earlier *Manchurian Candidate* in particular. He is anesthetised for the surgical conversion from Hamilton to Wilson and, at the end of it all, is given a strong relaxant under restraint prior to his final fate at the hands of the Cadaver Procurement Section.

Nicotine is present as stress companion for Hamilton and social component for Wilson. Beyond cigarettes, Hamilton's days of recreational intoxication appear to be over, if they had ever begun; the bottle of what we might suppose to be sleeping pills or maybe Valium (which had been introduced to the American market in 1963) on his bedside table is the only visible suggestion of self-administered drugs. Apart from someone smoking a joint at the grape stomp, there is nothing recreational about the drug-taking in *Seconds*, and what is consumed is often administered without consent and falls squarely in the category of 'downers' rather than 'uppers'.

Another drug, namely alcohol – a socially sanctioned, legally endorsed drug in the 1960s, especially for those of privilege in American society such as a Harvard graduate – makes a special contribution to *Seconds*. Whereas the dispensing of wine at the grape stomp festival lubricates Wilson's inhibitions and allows him to be positively Reborn, the consumption of alcohol at his cocktail party takes any newfound liberation to extreme lengths and, in fact, causes him to regress to his former self. The revelations of this scene mean we could consider the 'rebirth' at the grape stomp in a different light: that of the reemergence of Arthur Hamilton. Once a genie has been let out of the bottle, everyone knows it cannot be put back in.[8]

In the grape stomp scene, they bang tambourines and blow on pipes and recorders to the song-in-a-round – a never-ending loop – of the popular sea shanty *Drunken Sailor*. Yet, the lyrics to this ditty are far more pertinent when applied to Wilson's behaviour at his cocktail party.

'What shall we do with the drunken sailor?'

If the actions of the other Reborns at the party are any indication, the answer is: get him away from everyone, hold him down and serve him some sobering truths.

Whereas the gathering starts with cocktail party sophistication and decorum, we instantly clock Wilson's intention to get hammered. He pays token acknowledgement to Nora's requests to slow down by tipping the contents of his glass on the floor, and then proceeds to do as he intends: drink more. The alcohol is the enabler that brings flashes of Arthur Hamilton to the fore. When Nora calls him a *'dirty old man'*, the older Hamilton in the younger Wilson reacts. When the party guest refers to her husband – a so-called lawyer from Harvard University – as a *'sneaky two-face'*, the Hamilton in Wilson can't help but laugh at the irony of it all. *'Is he really a sneaky two-face?'* Wilson is getting an inkling of the real identities of his party guests.

As Wilson becomes more inebriated, the camera reflects his state, and takes on the more rollicking, rolling movements of the grape stomp. At a couple of points, we can figuratively see the monkey on his back, the static camera attached to him, similar to that of the '34 Lafayette St.' messenger in the opening Grand Central Station scene.

With the progression of the party and Wilson's intoxication, the music also becomes more frantic, in a 1960s go-go style. Wilson cannot let the Harvard reference slide, and he tries to question his guest about his supposed Harvard connections. Then Wilson starts talking about other aspects of Arthur Hamilton's life and, despite the glares of his guests and their insistence for him to stop, the alcohol has unleashed a beast that he can no longer contain. Whereas drugs were once used to control Hamilton/Wilson, he now uses alcohol to break his chains.

The dichotomy of alcohol consumption – the extremes of emotions that can start with joy then turn so quickly to despair and vice versa – is used here to demonstrate how no one person can exist without the co-existence of these polar opposite emotions. There is joy in Wilson that he has Nora to love and the promise of something fresh and new but there is also deep mourning for who he once was. In becoming a Reborn and hoping for the grass to be greener on the other side, he has made the profound realisation that nothing actually changes. When the male party guests drag Wilson into the other room and pin him to the bed, he calls for Nora. She bursts in, and brings her anger with her:

'Damn you! Just who the hell do you think you are?'[9]

He doesn't answer but, if he did, we know what the answer would be: Arthur Hamilton.

Notes

1. Of course, 'the Change' is also a euphemism for the menopause and, to a lesser extent the male menopause, the official NHS definition of which reads like a character sketch of Arthur Hamilton:
   'Some men develop depression, loss of sex drive, erectile dysfunction, and other physical and emotional symptoms when they reach their late 40s to early 50s. Other symptoms common in men this age are:
   - mood swings and irritability
   - loss of muscle mass and reduced ability to exercise
   - fat redistribution, such as developing a large belly or "man boobs" (gynaecomastia)
   - a general lack of enthusiasm or energy
   - difficulty sleeping (insomnia) or increased tiredness
   - poor concentration and short-term memory

   The 'male menopause': https://www.nhs.uk/conditions/male-menopause/
   These symptoms can interfere with everyday life and happiness, so it's important to find the underlying cause and work out what can be done to resolve it.'

2. Within two years of the pill's release in 1960, it was being used by 1.2 million American women: https://www.theguardian.com/society/2007/sep/12/health.medicineandhealth

3. On 29th August 1966, the Beatles played their final live arena concert at San Francisco's Candlestick Park. After performing their closing song, 'Long Tall Sally', the band was whisked away from the stage in the back of a 'meat wagon' (a popular slang term for a police van) for their own safety. Beatles lore suggests that this was the moment that precipitated their 'change' to an ostensibly studio-based band, reappearing as they did nine months later in the form of Sgt. Pepper's Lonely Hearts Club Band. 1966 was also the year of the notoriously recalled 'butcher cover' artwork for their US compilation album release 'Yesterday and Today', featuring the Fab Four dressed in white coats and draped with pieces of meat and doll body parts. Any relation to the themes discussed in this book relating to *Seconds* is purely coincidental.

4. The renowned Swedish artist, filmmaker and occultist Magister Carl Abrahamsson names *Seconds* as one of his favourite films: https://www.churchofsatan.com/the-black-flame-infernal-resonances-a/

5. For the crew, shooting this grape stomp scene was a confronting process. Salome Jens admits to feeling 'ridiculous' and an 'outcast' for gatecrashing such an event with their film unit. Frankenheimer reveals that the older, more conservative cinematographer James Wong Howe outright refused to get into the vat with these naked and overly enthusiastic festivalgoers, so Frankenheimer shot the scene himself in a number of loose, hand-held shots with the help of their young camera assistant, John Alonso. Frankenheimer also

acknowledges his editor, David Newhouse, for taking the many filmed fragments of this scene and bringing them together in a profound, seamless whole, including post-synch dialogue.

6. In his Criterion DVD commentary, Frankenheimer says the original theatrical version of *Seconds* was edited upon insistence by the Catholic Church; however, he believes the edit made the scene look more like an orgy, whereas the full version shows that it's just a group of people jumping around having a good time.

7. Salome Jens anecdotally recalls the filming of the grape stomp scene:

    'The grapes didn't arrive... There were 80 tonnes of grapes that were arriving from Texas... because of the crop that year had been very bad so they didn't have grapes. Now, the people who were doing the grapes stomp only wanted the grapes. They didn't want to be paid but they wanted the grapes to make wine. So, we couldn't shoot the scene unless the grapes arrived. And of course, there was this incredible worry that the grapes wouldn't arrive in time to pull the shoot too.

    'They've got this huge bath that they have to pull all these grapes and then of course people get into that bath and then they have to say, "Stomp that grape!" And I said to Frankenheimer, "That's the scene? I'm going to get in that grape bath with Rock and with these people and we're going to say, 'Stomp that grape?' This is the most ridiculous thing I've ever heard. I'm not going to do this. This will not work. This is silly." And I feel embarrassed because they're so beautiful. These are beautiful people.

    'Anyway, he says, "It's $10 million. You've got to get in there. You got to do it. You got to do it." Anyway, it starts getting dark and we began, it's time to do that dancing. He is in a bathing suit and everybody else is covered up except for these wonderful people who outright got started jumping in that bath. And the grapes have arrived and, of course, they are jumping in there. And I said, "Fine." I said to him, "Look, I'm going to get in there but just once. So just be ready..."

    'So the time came and I threw off that dress and jumped into that bath and started splashing grapes all over the place. I mean, I kept moving the grapes so that I was throwing grapes at everybody, and we were laughing and throwing grapes so that you could hardly see me. I was covered.

    'Then they threw Rock in and he was... I grabbed the whole of him and I wouldn't let him go. I just pulled him to my chest and I stayed on his chest the whole time and it was just getting crazy, laughter and insanity. And it worked. Afterwards, Frankenheimer said, "You know, you made that scene work and I really ought to thank you." But as I say, it came out of the madness of the moment. I had no idea what was going to happen. And finally, it was out of that insane, fun that we made of it that the scene worked.' (Interview with co-author)

8. Rock Hudson famously got drunk during the shooting of this scene so he could perform it

with full authenticity.

9. Salome Jens says of her delivery of this line:

    'The first run through with it, I did it very emotionally and [John Frankenheimer] said, "I really want you to take out the emotion. I don't want emotion. I want hard." And I said, "Oh God, John. How can we get through this movie finding that this relationship is evolving and have it be that cold. I think that she falls in love with him." And he said, "I don't want that. I don't want her with any kind of self-pity." So I said, "I beg you, I just beg you. I fear it's going to be very detrimental to the film."

    So John came up with a compromise, "Oh, I'll tell you what we'll do," he said, "We'll shoot it your way and then we'll shoot it mine." And, of course, when I saw it, he was absolutely right because certainly, the hard way [of saying the line] was much more loving actually than if I had sentimentalised it. So, of course, he used his way and I was certainly glad that he prevailed because he was right.' (Interview with co-author)

SOUND | VISION: 'Of course, the photography is not too professional... but I think it's clear enough'

'How puzzling all these changes are! I'm never sure what I'm going to be, from one minute to another.' – Lewis Carroll, *Alice's Adventures in Wonderland*

Seconds mirrored the times in which it was made. It did not, however, provide a comfortable mirror image; its contemporary audiences, such as they were, looked upon it and flinched much as Wilson flinches, struggling to come to terms with his new appearance when first confronted with a reflective surface after the surgical bandages have been removed to reveal his new face.

The image that each of us sees when we look at ourselves in a mirror is a distortion of reality, even if the surface of the mirror is level and entirely lacking in curvature, magnification or impediment. You see a flipped version of your face, in truth the opposite to the 'you' that others see. Yet, it is the 'you' that you carry around in your own mind and the 'you' that you spend time convincing yourself is what others take you for.

In most cases, anyone taking a selfie will initially see the mirror image of themselves on their screen, the familiar, comfortable and favoured version that they have grown used to over many years of gazing upon a reflection of themselves. The 'is that me?' feeling of seeing the resultant photograph with all of its asymmetrical difference, the face that others see, can be a little jarring and uncomfortable. We encounter a similar phenomenon when we listen to a recording of our own voice. There's the voice that you hear, the one that travels out of your mouth and back into your ears but also reverberates internally within your head, then there's the voice that others hear and which you only get to hear by way of recorded audio playback transmitted through a speaker.

Wilson gets to experience this sensation in the film. We learn that his surgery has altered his speaking voice: *'We've extracted all your teeth and given you a complete vocal cord resection,'* the Company surgeon informs him. When he hears his own new voice played back on Davalo's tape recording, it's bound to sound like somebody else but even his pre-surgical Arthur Hamilton voice would have sounded a little odd to him. Through sound and vision (although let's not forget the second division senses of smell, touch and taste), we construct our perception of reality and 'make sense' of the world around us. Richard Gregory's 'top down' theory of visual perception asserts that the sense we make of things is formed around existing knowledge or expectations; essentially our experience of living and being provides us with a complex set of accrued coordinates on which we base our recognition of immediate reality (MacLeod 2018).

A commonly used illustration of this is an optical illusion in the form of a three-dimensional cast of a face or a mask. When the eye looks upon the concave aspect of the cast, the brain – based on memory and pattern recognition – perceives a convex face. We're compelled to try to understand what we see based on what we expect to see. *Seconds* shows us a character in Hamilton/Wilson whose issues with self-recognition go way beyond any normal 'is that me?' moment. The surgical procedure elicits, on first sight, a reaction that smacks of full-blown 'that's not me!' No matter how much Hamilton must have been aware of the drastic nature of the physical change he signed up for, we aren't privy to any scenes where he is shown a preview of his new face. The most we see are the 'blueprints' that guide the surgeons through the operation, so we have no sense that Hamilton knew absolutely what he was going to look like.

Mirrors and mirroring play an important role in *Seconds* – from the triptych of mirrors on the reveal of Wilson to his panic attack in the airline bathroom – that is literally and thematically established in the opening credits with the Bass' rendering of facial parts in mirrors that are then pulled and twisted into awkward shapes. At several points throughout the film, Hamilton/Wilson is presented with his mirror image, which serves the purpose of him 'reflecting' on himself physically and spiritually. Does he recognise that which he sees in the mirror? Does the external image represent the internal reality? If it didn't as Hamilton, then it still doesn't as Wilson. As such, the film offers more than simply a depiction of its protagonist experiencing his own radical physical change. Through its cinematography, sound and editing choices, it stimulates a physical response in the viewer that is entirely in keeping with the predicament of Hamilton/Wilson. Its signature assemblage of jarring, cutting, blurring and bending of the image can leave the body of the viewer responding involuntarily.

Films that work hard to generate a physical reaction in those watching them are, of course, commonplace. We often can't help acquiring a lump in the throat during emotional scenes, gripping on to the armrests tight during perilous moments, putting our hands in front of our eyes or jumping out of our skin while watching horror films, even becoming uncomfortably aware of the discomfort of our seat when we find a film thoroughly disengaging. We're being manipulated, emotionally, perceptually, cognitively. It's what cinema has done since the advent of the edit. Filmmakers direct the viewer's mind, determining and establishing their responses, deliberately pushing buttons to provoke a response. *Seconds* pushes the envelope by striving to trigger an instinctive reflex through its 'flick book' approach to visual and aural juxtaposition.

It brings to mind a similarly under-appreciated film by Czech New Wave surrealist Pavel Juráček, *A Case for a Rookie Hangman* (1970). Drawing from Jonathan Swift's *Gulliver's Travels* – and ornamented with familiar elements from Lewis Carroll's 'Alice's Adventures in Wonderland' (e.g. a well-dressed hare with pocket-watch)[1] – Juráček's magnificently augmented film hangs on far looser narrative threads than Frankenheimer's film yet, through its distorted, contorted black and white visuals, it creates a potent political/personal message with more than an edge of paranoia that could come straight out of the *Seconds* playbook.

Given Frankenheimer's repeated use of lulling shots followed by sudden cuts and blasts of sound, the physical jolts that we sustain in *Seconds* are reminiscent of the only partially understood phenomenon of hypnic jerks, sometimes referred to as myoclonic twitches; those moments when we approach the sleep state only to semi-dream about, for example, missing a step and falling forward, resulting usually in waking up with a start. Myoclonus is any kind of sudden, involuntary and uncontrollable muscle contraction or relaxation, the most common example being the hiccup.

The jolts of *Seconds* aren't the jump scares of horror cinema; they are the missed steps, the sudden drops and the resulting caught breath of our reflex responses and, collectively over the course of the film, they contribute hugely to its grip of isolation.

CONSTELLATIONS

In the field of neuroscience, mirror neurons are a relatively recent discovery. As applied to cinema, they can explain the overwhelming sense of immersion that a film can impose on a viewer. In wider behavioural terms, mirror neurons are behind those almost unstoppable physical responses to certain sights and situations that may, on the face of it, seem to serve little practical purpose. For example, you might be walking along, and a person with a pronounced limp comes into view. You might then find yourself experiencing the (literally) knee-jerk compulsion to affect a similar limp – that's your mirror neurons kicking in whether you like it or not. It's an experience that is likely to have occurred several times over the course of your life and, each time, it may have led to a fair degree of guilty soul-searching – 'why am I instinctively mimicking a disabled person?' – so it may come as a relief to know it is a neurological reaction, and one based on empathy rather than cruelty.

Possibly a more commonly experienced occurrence happens when you are in the presence of somebody who is carrying a heavy or unstable load – a precarious tower of plates perhaps or an overburdened tray. If the carrier stumbles leading to the potential dropping of an item, it's very common for a nearby observer to instinctively outstretch their hands in an approximated, but ultimately useless, catch gesture. The Italian neuroscientist Victorio Gallese, who was among those who discovered motor neurons in the early 1990s, holds a particular interest in their relationship to cinema. He helped to establish the theory of 'embodied simulation' to account for those moments when events on the screen before us trigger an involuntary response, body combining with mind in an empathic motor-sensorial reflection. Hitchcock's films were replete with such triggering moments; to test the theory, try watching the scene in *Strangers on a Train* (1951) when Bruno Antony (Robert Walker) reaches down through the grated inlet of a storm drain in an attempt to retrieve the incriminating monogrammed cigarette lighter that he has dropped, and notice what your own hands do when his fingertips are straining to reach the lighter. We can't help ourselves.

Seconds can feel like a mirror neuron-triggering rollercoaster at times. There is repeated use of the 'flinch jump cut' to suggest discomfort, sometimes social as seen in the jarring mix of shots showing Hamilton's sweaty discomposure on the commuter train, sometimes physical such as Wilson's initial recoil at first sight of his new post-operative face in the mirror. The effect is frequently achieved through a melding of camerawork and physical performance, and in this respect it is interesting to compare the bookend sequences of the film. The body-mounted camera rig shots in Grand Central Station hold the physicality of the actor as the unmoving locus of attention with the rest of the world left to shock-absorb the hectic motion. Contrast this with the locked-off shot looking down at Wilson struggling against the gurney restraints as he is wheeled into surgery at the end. Now the head of the protagonist is entirely trapped and left to rattle manically around the frame as effectively the only moving object within it. What these visual/sensory opposites share is the generation of involuntary disquiet in the viewer. Neither is entirely comfortable, smooth. Whether it be the person or the world that 'controls' our view, one serves, in frame, to accentuate the chaos of the other and vice versa. Furthermore, the grape stomp scene at around the half-way point in the film's run time presents the moment when both person and world align in a shared state, that of pandemonium. Despite this 'harmony' the mad whirl of imagery leads the viewer to involuntarily experience the total loss of stasis, a little like watching the film while tethered to a rapidly rotating merry-go-round spun by another's hand. This whole journey of order and chaos both playing against one another and combining owes a great deal to the inventiveness of James Wong Howe.

In championing the film's visual technicalities, *American Cinematographer* magazine accordingly attributes Frankenheimer's decision to enlist the 67-year-old Wong Howe as director of photography as one of the film production's defining moments:

> 'A seasoned Hollywood professional who always sought to bend the rules and express a story in vivid visual terms, Howe was a perfect collaborator for the youthful and ambitious Frankenheimer.'

> 'The camera is not merely a recording device in *Seconds*, but an expressive tool. By pushing conventional technique aside and working with a visual grammar of exaggeration and extreme graphic amplification, Howe and Frankenheimer revealed the mind of a man struggling to break free of his emotional bonds 14 years before Martin Scorsese and director of photography Michael Chapman, ASC, would similarly attempt to capture the black-and-white torment of Jake LaMotta in

Raging Bull.' (LoBrutto 2018)

Indeed, in the DVD commentary for the film, Frankenheimer himself also concedes that Wong Howe's contribution to the film was immense, more than any other cameraman with which he would collaborate.

By the time he shot *Seconds*, Wong Howe was one of the most accomplished cinematographers in Hollywood, particularly in the black and white medium (*Seconds* being the last monochrome film he would lens). His career was already entering its fifth decade by 1966, having started as a cinematographer on the 1922 silent film *Drums of Destiny* (or *Drums of Fate*, as it is alternatively known). *American Cinematographer* describes Wong Howe's style as 'deep-focus photography, low-key moods, film noir; and naturalistic, romantic and expressive lighting effects' – all of which are given a stunning showcase in *Seconds*, and resulted in an Oscar nomination, one of nine during his long career (he won twice, for *The Rose Tattoo* in 1956 and *Hud* in 1964). On the night of the *Seconds* nomination he lost out to Haskell Wexler for *Who's Afraid of Virginia Woolf?*

Opinion is divided over whether it was Wong Howe or Frankenheimer who elected to use an extremely wide 9.7mm lens to shoot the film. Regardless of who was behind this decision, this choice of lens proved to be integral to the style of *Seconds* and, without it, we would be speaking about a very different film. As Frankenheimer said to film critic Gerald Pratley in 1969:

> 'In *Seconds*, the [idea of] distortion was terribly important. The distortion of what society had made this man, what the Company then turned him out to be, and finally when he was going to his death everything had to be that complete distortion of reality and the fact that it was all just utter nonsense.' (Pratley 1969: 135)

Distortion throughout the film comes in the form of wide angles, courtesy of the 9.7mm fisheye lens and its central distorted view, as well as low angles, which had already become a hallmark of Frankenheimer's directing style. Added to this, all manner of unconventional, often uncomfortable camera placement was put to use, which posed many challenges for the shooting process. Multiple cameras were used simultaneously; for example four were employed to capture Hamilton's 'lovemaking' with his wife. This required a high-level of 'choreography' from the operators in order to avoid any one of them entering the others' frames. Cameras were wedged in suitcases, such as during the opening walk through Grand Central Station. At other times the crew resorted to hand-held cameras. You will find examples of this in the scene showing Hamilton the commuter on the train home to Scarsdale from Grand Central Station, and also very noticeably throughout the grape stomping scene in Santa Barbara. This particular technique was cumbersome and physically exhausting given the large Arriflex film stock cameras of the time. These cameras were also very loud, which meant that during scenes in which the camera is right in the thick of the action, for example during the cocktail party breakdown at Wilson's Malibu house, dialogue needed to be post-looped due to intrusive camera noise.

Seconds employed a camera mount very similar in principle to what is now known as 'SnorriCam', named after Icelandic photographers the Snorri Brothers who worked with numerous indie film directors in the 1990s, notably Darren Aronofsky whose debut feature *Pi* (1997) employed the rig to great effect. SnorriCam mounts tether to the chest and shoulders of the actor to create the effect of the performer remaining absolutely still within the frame while the background moves around them. The effect is that of wooziness, a sense of disorientation, that could be used to communicate panic or anxiety, or that of being under the influence of drugs or alcohol. In *Seconds*, coupled with an 18mm lens, it is used to convey all of the above. You will find it employed in the film for those aforementioned shots in Grand Central Station as well as during Wilson's disastrous cocktail party.

The use of the body-mounted camera is significant in *Seconds* because, although not the first film to use it – the banned left-wing German film *Kuhle Wampe* (Slatan Dudow, 1932) was an early example of its application – this camera technique was definitely unusual for 1966, so its inclusion sticks out, in a positive sense, like a stylistic sore thumb, another highly effective mode of distortion that fits neatly into *Seconds*' thematic brief. Film audiences today are more likely to be familiar with the woozy aesthetic thanks to Harvey Keitel's drunken walk through the bar in Martin Scorsese's *Mean Streets* (1973), a number of somnambulistic scenes in Aronofsky's more widely seen follow-up to *Pi*, *Requiem for a Dream* (2000) and across a host of TV shows such as *Lost*, *Scrubs*, *Dexter* and *Shameless*. In wider society the micro-shrinkage of technology has led to bodycam devices routinely worn by law-enforcement officers, producing footage that is frequently consumed by audiences of news programming, crime documentaries and the like, making the experience of seeing body-mounted camera footage very commonplace nowadays. For *Seconds* to pull it off so successfully when it did, long before lightweight cameras and mounts were available, shows just want a ground-breaking film it was, at the very least from a technical perspective.

It is difficult to imagine *Seconds* without Wong Howe's signature style: his deep focus. Deep focus is the use of lenses that capture a large depth of field so the entire shot composition – fore, middle and background – remains in perfect focus. Wong Howe exploited this technique superbly in *Seconds*, emphasising every aspect of the *mise-en-scène* and turning every frame into a mini-masterpiece.

The combination of direction, art direction and cinematography in *Seconds* results in a rather cluttered frame but one from which intense beauty is derived, and one that reveals more and more detail with every viewing of the film. Wong Howe and Frankenheimer intelligently direct our attention with subtle shifts of camera focus, artfully constructing each frame as a perfect singular composition nestled within the overarching narrative, almost a story-within-a-story. It is a heady experience to behold, and one that enables *Seconds* to turn quotidian moments into something incredibly rich and illuminating.[2]

This brilliance notwithstanding, the filmmakers' influences shine as bright as the operating theatre lights in the film's final moments. The French New Wave had a major impact on the visual storytelling by flying in the face of hitherto traditional filmmaking methods, freeing the camera from presupposed 'rules' (including being shackled to a tripod) and embracing visual and narrative distortion to reflect differing states of mind. Frankenheimer, being the Francophile that he was, it is no surprise to see this emerging aesthetic pushing through into his work. Combine this with the documentary/live television methods of his earlier work, and you achieve a result that, according to *American Cinematographer* 'looks like a *Twilight Zone* episode directed by Jean-Luc Godard' (LoBrutto 2018).

Not only did the subject matter and Frankenheimer's vision lend itself beautifully to Wong Howe as an artistic visionary but, just like Rock Hudson, Wong Howe – a Chinese national by birth (he was born Wong Tung Jim in Guangdong in 1899) – was living a double life, one public and one private. He defied California's antimiscegenation laws by dating author Sanora Babb – a white woman – marrying her in France in 1937, although their marriage was not legally recognised in the USA until laws against interracial marriage were abolished. Wong Howe's own conservatism and the 'morals clause' of his studio contract also meant they could neither live together nor publicly acknowledge their union, a situation similar to Rock Hudson's forced closeting of his sexuality.

If this was not enough to draw Wong Howe to *Seconds*, McCarthyism and the House of Un-American Activities Committee hearings affected him directly. Specifically, Babb and Wong Howe's relationship endured further stress on top of the institutionalised racism when Babb placed herself in self-imposed exile in Mexico with other blacklisted Hollywood creatives. Given her beliefs and the era's political witch-hunt, she came to this decision of her own accord to protect her husband's career from potentially damaging controversy.

The beauty of filmmaking as a collective form means that, as important as Wong Howe and Frankenheimer's input may be, theirs was not the only input that brought *Seconds* to life. Art director Ted Haworth accentuated Wong Howe and Frankenheimer's visual ambitions with a spatially fluid set design that worked intuitively with the exaggeration of the camera lensing. While some sets were presented in normal proportions then warped through the camera's wide angles, others were distorted in perspective and shot with normal lenses. One such distorted set is seen when Hamilton drinks the tea offered to him by the Company, leading him 'through the looking-glass' and into an an unwitting sexual embrace with an unknown woman. As *American Cinematographer* explains:

> 'The room's heavily textured walls raked at extreme angles to create a false sense of perspective, while the floor undulated beneath black-and-white checkerboard tiles. Exemplified by this scene, the physical and optical distortion achieved by Haworth's sets and Howe's cinematography combined throughout *Seconds* to

create a disturbing, stomach-churning effect of a Kafkaesque universe.' (LoBrutto 2018)

Frankenheimer also paid tribute to the excellent work of his editor, David Newhouse – specifically the grape stomping scene where the mishmash of hand-held imagery, which could have been lost in the moment, is given narrative lucidity in the cutting room. Contrastingly, the whole scene where the 'friendly' Company boss convinces Hamilton to sign the contract was completed in just two takes, giving Newhouse no opportunity to cut away in the editing or provide an alternate version of the scene.

Jerry Goldsmith's foreboding music accentuates the visuals of *Seconds* with an aural accompaniment that is a perfect match and arguably one of Goldsmith's best film scores. Despite his compositions being neither distorted, atonal nor avant-garde, his music serves as a genuine complement, rather than counterpoint, to the piercing vision of the film; highly musical and emotive but in a way that stays with you. He employs melancholic orchestral strings and piano in minor keys but then also dips into heavy, sustained chords on the pipe organ in order to make a gothic statement, as if welcoming the Phantom of the Opera (such parallels to a character grappling with the incongruence between his internal self and external appearance should not be ignored). The drama of the organ is used to its best funereal effect during the Company's surgical procedure where it recalls the sense of a mad scientist in his laboratory dancing with the Devil. Indeed, these Company employees are performing God's work, an act that assumes serious consequences and, therefore, deserves to be underscored with appropriate gravity.

Seconds is very much all about its constituent parts. The various body parts that are subdivided and reconfigured by the Company surgeons could be considered proxies for the multitudinous production elements that were pulled together in the film's making. Despite the serious excellence of its contributors and the wonderful work that they brought to the project, it can be regarded as a film on the whole that is rather *less* than the sum of its parts, less of a mirror held up to society in an attempt to reflect the issues of the times in which it was made, more of a mirror-ball, dazzling but fragmentary and ephemeral, serving only to scatter its commentary and make the experience of watching the film unnecessarily and unsatisfactorily discomforting and difficult. While there is some foundation to this verdict, it fails to acknowledge that this disintegration was consciously written into the film's DNA – it is *meant* to be jarring and problematic and is deliberately so in the conscious pursuit of a visceral response from its audience. More than that, the concerted process of gathering up these distributed pieces brings its own 'reward' for those willing to do so: a deeper, richer psychological reception and appreciation of the film. To quote Rod Serling's introduction to every episode of *The Twilight Zone*, that television series to which *Seconds* is frequently and not entirely kindly likened, the film exists in 'a dimension not only of sight and sound but of mind.'

Notes

1. The influence of *Alice's Adventures in Wonderland* can also be seen in the drug-induced sexual molestation scene in *Seconds*. It is important to note the appeal of Lewis Carroll's tale on the 1960s psychedelia counterculture (e.g. Jefferson Airplane's iconic, 'White Rabbit' from the aptly title album released in 1967, *Surrealistic Pillow*). That which was 'trippy' or dreamlike often led 'through the looking-glass'.
2. One such example of this is the old man in the laundry who offhandedly informs Hamilton of the change in address (a veteran TV actor, according to Frankenheimer). Despite his brief appearance, he lingers long in our consciousness, in part due to the superb composition of the shots in which he appears that prompt us to want to know more about him: Does he too work for the Company? What does he know of the clandestine practices that he is helping to facilitate? Does he not approve? Is that why they no longer operate through his laundry?

WORK / CONSUME / DIE: 'The years I've spent, trying to get all the things I was told were important, that I was supposed to want'

Perhaps, some day, people will look at the metal and paper in their pockets and realise it means nothing, and if they all agreed to agree that it meant nothing, we could all just head to the beach and watch the waves come in. – Frankie Boyle, *Work! Consume! Die!*

Seconds is a film that offers no hope. Critics often flail when expounding on their disparagements of why *Seconds* does not work. When they talk of the film being uncomfortable in its visual contortions or neglecting to sell the transmogrification of the protagonist from John Randolph to Rock Hudson, their justifications are predominantly flimsy. *Seconds* is a masterstroke of surreality, with imagery that holds up to Buñuelian standards of the form, and its handling of the central 'character reassignment' requires little in the way of suspension of belief or theatricality to sell such a premise. Rather than own the fact that *Seconds* is possibly not to their taste, many critics overlook the hopelessness of the film, and how the lack of possibility or removal of any 'narrative sunrise' makes it a very difficult watch and, consequently, unpalatable for certain viewers – film critics or otherwise. This does not make it a quantifiably bad or flawed film, but to be hopeless is a form of storytelling suicide. For the filmmakers to believe *Seconds* could rise above such inherent dourness and secure significant audience numbers was somewhat naïve. The film was arguably doomed to nosedive at the box office and among critics. It needed to soften over time and inch slowly into the film-viewing consciousness before it could be fully appreciated.

That *Seconds* was made without any alterations to its conclusion is something of a miracle. The finality of Wilson's journey – without any recourse (he is definitely going to die this time), without absolution (even the 'holy man' who accompanies him on his final journey is unable to satisfactorily perform last rites) or without redemption (despite his cosmetic alterations, Hamilton/Wilson fails to mature or progress as a human being) – is utterly soul-destroying for viewers to bear witness, especially those who may be struggling with their own existential conundrum. In other words, *Seconds* does not let its audience off lightly. We are presented with a cycle of life that would be acutely familiar to many people – work, consume, die. Within this cycle, we all search for meaning across the courses of our existence, regardless of our socio-economic status, although many will find hope in the slim chance of eventually realising The American Dream, whether that comes through hard work or hitting the lotto jackpot.

Seconds doesn't even give us that hope; it takes a white man of social standing and fortune, and startlingly demonstrates how even he – the top of the social pile – cannot rise above his state of hopelessness. We're not even given glimpses of past moments of joy that we might assume he would have experienced; his wedding day, the birth of his daughter, promotions at work. Arthur Hamilton is a man mired in gloom who appears to have never enjoyed a modicum of happiness across his entire life. *Seconds* is definitive in its prognosis that we all work, consume then die, regardless of our material worth and privilege. Human existence is nothing more than that.

Another popular filmmaker working at that time, Billy Wilder, was known for his bleak narratives and profound reflections on the human condition. His film, *The Apartment* (1960), offered a similar commentary on the work-consume-die cycle, albeit one that is played out through a far more sincere love story, whereas the 'love story' of *Seconds* is nothing more than collateral damage from Hamilton/Wilson's Company-supplied persona. Jack Lemmon's character of C.C. Baxter in *The Apartment* is doomed to the rinse-and-repeat cycle of his existence as 'some schnook who works in the office' of an insurance company, Consolidated Life of New York. Regardless of whether loaning his apartment to the firm's executives for extramarital trysts results in him getting a promotion or not, he will always be one refusal away from demotion back to the corporate trenches from where he came.

Baxter's desk (Ordinary Policy Department, Premium Accounting Division, 19th floor, Section W, number 861) is positioned within a massive expanse of desks, all lined up perfectly in rows with the click-clacking of typewriters creating a monotonous thrum against the home office cohort of 31,259 employees (the quoting of such figures opens the film and, importantly, helps establish the corporate numbers game from the outset). Other than a gormless chap sitting beside him, who bemoans Baxter being first to get a promotion, he and his fellow insurance workers function as a largely nameless mass – the working class – battery hens in a soulless organisation where they are fed pipe-dreams of opportunities that will never manifest. While Arthur Hamilton's working day in *Seconds* places him in a position of authority – as unsatisfactory as that may still be – it is only through his 'recruitment' into the Company that he experiences a reality similar to Baxter's working life; in the day room with the other failed Reborns where he is expected to take to the phone and, in medicated servitude, sell the proposition of a new life to his former companions; a kind of callous twist on the pyramid or party-plan selling model. This Company, in fact, flourishes on its failures; without them, it would have no future customers.

In Wilder's, and his cinematographer Joseph LaShelle's, presentation of their office phone room, we can see where *Seconds* owes a stylistic debt – the heavy geometric lines of the office ceiling in *The Apartment* narrowing back into the background to create an optical illusion of infinity; of something that will never end. In *Seconds*, there are a number of points where geometry and patterns create a prism (or 'prison'?) in the frame, within which the characters are enclosed or where the 'weight' of the geometry bears down formidably from above them. Consider the scene we've explored in a previous chapter, where a pre-Wilson Hamilton is in the bedroom with his wife and – through the composition, framing and lighting of these shots – we instantly feel the enormous burden Hamilton carries on his shoulders.

In *The Apartment*, Wilder and I.A.L. Diamond's storyline uses the counterpoint of Christmas as backdrop to Fran Kubelik's suicide attempt (played by Shirley MacLaine). As the white-gloved elevator girl at Baxter's firm, and the dumped mistress of a cuckolding executive, Fran sees no escape from her work-consume-die cycle than to shortcut to 'die' by consuming a bottle of sleeping pills. Her affair with Jeff D. Sheldrake (Fred MacMurray), and his promises of love and a future together, fed her with hope that she was destined for something better. When taken away, there is nothing for her to live for. The ending of *The Apartment* offers a trick-of-the-mind where Fran awakens from the fog of her ennui; she realises Sheldrake will never change and 'the good guy', C.C. Baxter, who has quit both his job and his apartment for the chance of something better, offers her a greater shot at happiness. She therefore runs into Baxter's arms where they live, we assume, happily ever after. But do they? *Can* they?

If we look beyond the grand romantic overtures and delve under the skin of the situation, it's difficult to imagine their work-consume-die cycle being broken. Does she really love Baxter or is he just the one who's there? Are they likely to have improved job prospects? And what is the probability of a working class man in 1960 being able to afford a decent home without employment? Just as Ben Braddock and Elaine Robinson stare blankly into an uncertain future from the back of a bus in the dying moments of *The Graduate* (Mike Nicholls 1967), if Wilder had allowed the finale of *The Apartment* to linger that little bit longer, things might not have looked so rosy.

Despite its dark undercurrent, *The Apartment* was a critically lauded instant classic, garnering 10 nominations at the 1961 Oscars, from which it took five wins including Best Picture, Best Director and Best Screenplay. While *Seconds* was not entirely overlooked by the awards circuit (James Wong Howe was rightfully nominated for an Oscar for his cinematography), the reception of *Seconds* when compared to that afforded *The Apartment* could not have been more different. Yet, both films tackle similar themes, present a cycle from which there is no escape, and offer a future that is just as scary or scarier than the present. The big difference is *The Apartment* sweetens its cheerlessness with a proven antidote: comedy. Even the most tasteless subject matter is made edible with a smattering of humour and, in folding comedy into the harsh realities of the human condition, Billy Wilder produced a film that gave evidence of his genius.

Seconds is no less a film than *The Apartment* but the avoidance of any humour, even humour that could be considered black, almost threatened the film's survival. The small moments of lightness – the 'chicken-picking' at the Company meeting, for instance ('They have a wonderful way of baking cheese on it so it's very crispy') – were unscripted, unintended distractions. *Seconds* was shamelessly courageous in its refusal to dilute its content to pander to an audience by making the viewing experience easier. But, even if hope is the patsy that lets viewers off the hook – or 'false hope', as is the case of *The Apartment* – it is the possibility of hope that people need and crave. When taken away, just like Fran Kubelick, there is nothing for us to live for. So it can be said that *Seconds* gives us nothing to live for. Worse, through its frankness, it shows us that the supposed hope that we are fed in other stories is merely a placebo.

One would assume the maker behind such a film as *Seconds* would be a pessimist. But Frankenheimer, a political beast, still had hope – at least at the time when *Seconds* was made. Not one but four of the actors in *Seconds* had previously been blacklisted: John Randolph, Will Geer, Jeff Corey and Nedrick Young.[2] The film signalled particularly Randolph's long-awaited return to Hollywood in the central role of Arthur Hamilton. As a friend of the Kennedy clan, Frankenheimer had also been badly affected by the assassination of JFK; however, he had another ace up his sleeve, and someone with whom he would become inextricably linked: Robert Francis Kennedy.

Robert Kennedy's inclusive populism that blurred racial lines – uniting working class whites with black voters – appealed greatly to Frankenheimer's political sensibilities. Subsequently, Frankenheimer accepted an invitation to shoot the promotional materials for RFK's 1968 presidential campaign, which he enacted in a highly progressive manner that clearly communicated Kennedy's (and Frankenheimer's) no-nonsense, non-elitist values. The black and white documentary style of Frankenheimer's television commercials (a medium in which he had cut his filmmaking teeth) showed Kennedy as a man of the people, noticeably devoid of hubris and political pettiness or mud-slinging. His campaign for Kennedy was one of stately pride, yet also of connectedness with 'the man on the street'. And it was a success. Hope was restored.

On Election Day, Tuesday 4th June 1968, Robert Kennedy relaxed with confidence of his victory at John Frankenheimer's Malibu home;[1] the same property that Rock Hudson as Tony Wilson inhabited in *Seconds*. According to investigative journalist and author Dan E. Moldea, Kennedy had become so relaxed he even suggested that he and his family and friends watch the primary results on the television in Malibu, rather than attend his own election party. However, given the assignment of the TV crews in Los Angeles, Kennedy begrudgingly headed into the city at 7.15pm, accompanied by John Frankenheimer and other members of his campaign team to the Ambassador Hotel, travelling in Frankenheimer's Rolls Royce Silver Cloud III.

What followed their arrival at the Ambassador is now indelibly recorded in US history. Stable boy Sirhan Sirhan, whose motivation as assassin remains unclear, fired four bullets into Kennedy when making a detour through the hotel kitchen following his victory speech. Frankenheimer's hopes for a brighter political future died along with Kennedy 26 hours later at the Good Samaritan Hospital.

Frankenheimer grappled with mental health issues, including alcoholism, in the aftermath of Kennedy's death, taking a sabbatical from filmmaking in France. In the opinion of some he never again hit the artistic heights of his pre-1968 career; while this remains a moot point, it is undeniable that he never worked at the speed or with the same passion as he did before Kennedy's death. In relaying those final moments at the Ambassador Hotel, photojournalist Bill Eppridge recalls an interaction with Frankenheimer:

> Like me, Frankenheimer was a native New Yorker, and I noticed that he referred to Kennedy as Bob, as I did. Where we came from, people named "Bobby" were either 9 years old or professional ballplayers. We talked a bit about the town that spawned us, and then about Frankenheimer's great paranoid masterwork from 1962, *The Manchurian Candidate*, which starred Frank Sinatra and Laurence Harvey. It had been withdrawn from public viewing after the killing of Jack Kennedy in 1963 (it would finally be rereleased in 1988). The story, based on a novel by Richard Condon, was about programming a man to assassinate a presidential candidate.
>
> "Do you think it could happen in what is laughingly called 'real life'?" I asked him.
>
> Frankenheimer smiled in a nervous way, and glanced at the door of the suite.
>
> "Yeah." (Eppridge 2008)

Frankenheimer's cinematic depiction of politics is that of apparent civility, underneath which simmers deception, betrayal and even violence that eventually belies any veil of diplomacy by boiling to the surface and erupting. True to the times, 'Frankenheimian' politics are the exclusive domain of men (correction: white men), although relegated to the role of 'first ladies', women could still act as puppet masters, as was so brilliantly enunciated to chilling effect by Angela Lansbury in *The Manchurian Candidate* and, to a lesser degree, Ava Gardner as the army general's ex-lover in *Seven Days in May* (she doesn't actively pull the strings but she has the power to trigger his downfall).

Arguably the most political of the films in Frankenheimer's 'Paranoia trilogy', *Seven Days in May* – as its name suggests – presents a week-long deadlock in Cold War-era American politics where well-liked army colonel Martin 'Jiggs' Casey (Kirk Douglas) uncovers a military plot to overthrow the US President Jordan Lyman (Fredric March) by his superior and mentor, General James Mattoon Scott (Burt Lancaster). This coup is incited by the President's decision to sign a nuclear disarmament treaty with the Soviet Union, which the army feels puts the United States at risk of a surprise attack.

Through even this brief synopsis, correlations between *Seven Days in May* and JFK's Cuban Missile Crisis of 1962 are strikingly apparent, as too is American hysteria over the Soviet threat that so heavily impacted the film industry with the now infamous Hollywood blacklist, of which Frankenheimer and his producer, Edward Lewis,[1] were demonstrable critics. It is a talk-heavy script (written by *The Twilight Zone*'s host and narrator, Rod Serling) that plays out in the hallowed hallways and genteel offices of the White House, through meetings of state, gentlemanly debate and handshakes. It is also a strident defence of the democracy upon which the American Constitution is so proudly based; a democracy that Frankenheimer sees as being under threat (or so we can gather from the cumulative content of his trilogy). *Seven Days in May* might have a lot to say about American politics but you don't necessarily hear it in the dialogue; you read it between the lines.

Scratch the surface of its conciliatory façade and the emptiness of the rhetoric is revealed – not that of political unity but of military overthrow. General Scott continually goads Casey, and the civility of his language and manner only makes the threat stronger. A righteous Casey – wanting to protect the government but also maintain his allegiance to his military superiors – finds himself seducing an emotionally unstable woman and then scrabbling desperately in her bin to retrieve Scott's love letters. As the nation's protector, he stoops low and is quite literally brought to his knees. Politics is a dirty business.

In *Seconds*, a new form of government is presented, that of the Company; a corporate, for-profit vessel that presides over its customers with the same level of contractual power as a head of state (i.e. they can even sanction your death, if deemed necessary). Compare the hyperbole of the Company to that of the public servants in *Seven Days in May* and you will note little difference. Both speak with a diplomatic tone of reassurance and practicality – essentially weasel words – that make everything appear supernormal but, as we see in both narratives, the actions of these Men of Power speak louder (and with greater honesty) than words.

It may be tempting to talk about *Seven Days in May* and *Seconds* in terms of their differences rather than likenesses but each informs the other in a very special way, as does *The Manchurian Candidate*. The three films, when cross-referenced and viewed together, function as a temperature check of the state of the Nation. As the film directly preceding *Seconds*, *Seven Days in May* also features a portion of dialogue that effectively provides the rationale for *Seconds*; the reason why someone like Arthur Hamilton can find no other means to escape his despondency. These words are the crowning monologue from Fredric March as the President in the concluding scenes of *Seven Days in May*:

> 'The enemy is an age, the nuclear age. It happens to have killed man's faith and his ability to influence what happens to him. Out of this comes a sickness; a sickness of frustration; a feeling of impotence, helplessness, weakness.'

Words such as 'frustration', 'impotence', 'helplessness' and 'weakness' are emasculating words; ones that describe Arthur Hamilton to a tee.

Frankenheimer was yet to know Robert Kennedy's fate when making *Seconds* but, prophetically, the Kennedy saga was written in *Seconds*' narrative. Just as the older Hamilton/younger Wilson try to break the cycle but are destined to follow an established continuum, so did the older Kennedy/younger Kennedy. Death on repeat. It is not so much that *Seconds* is cosmically prophetic but rather that it speaks an elemental truth of mortal existence. The work-consume-die paradigm is broad enough in its scope to apply to so many circumstances, across so many cultures.

It is something we can all see in ourselves and, in terms of its cyclical nature, can be applied even beyond death in Eastern philosophies through the concept of reincarnation.

It is a cycle that finds much expression through the creative arts. As aforementioned, in cinema, *The Apartment* deals with such a cycle, as does Harold Ramis' *Groundhog Day* (1993), a popular comedy that toys with the conceit of the same day relived on a seemingly never-ending loop as experienced by a weary, cynical working man, which was so influential that its title has now found a place in modern parlance to refer to a repeated experience. The landmark science fiction film of the same decade as *Seconds*, Stanley Kubrick's monumental *2001: A Space Odyssey* (1968), is ostensibly a depiction of the guided journey of the entire human race in general, from the Dawn of Man to the birth of the Star Child, and the life, death and rebirth of astronaut Dave Bowman (Kier Dullea) in particular.

There is also a sense of ending at the point of arrival in the final moments of that other milestone science fiction movie made in the immediate wake of *Seconds*, Franklin J, Schaffner's *Planet of the Apes* (1968). The broken remnants of the Statue of Liberty bring home the horrible realisation for astronaut George Taylor (Charlton Heston) that what he thought was an alien planet is in fact a future Earth. He never really left. There is something fittingly final about the placing of the statue, and this scene, on a beach. Early life crawled from the sea onto the land, and for humanity that liminal space between solid and liquid has always exerted an existential prospect of some kind of redemptive return to the source. Perhaps it represents the place where we might find out where we went wrong so that we can begin again, all new, all different. It is no coincidence that the final destination of the father and son in Cormac McCarthy's 2006 post-apocalyptic novel *The Road*, and its 2009 screen adaptation directed by John Hillcoat, is the ocean – the place of origin offering the possibility of deliverance.

The role of the shoreline in *Seconds* is completely consistent with this notion of a location that is apart from the world and therefore ideal for potential escape and rebirth. In the 1970s, it was a place that became synonymous with the very real male mid-life escape attempt of a prominent British politician. On November 20th

1974, the troubled 49-year-old Labour MP for Walsall North John Stonehouse left his clothes in a pile on a Miami beach, where it was initially assumed he had either committed suicide, accidentally drowned or possibly been the victim of a shark attack. Given the failure to discover a body, together with Stonehouse's known parlous financial situation, doubts came to be cast on his apparent fate. Around five weeks later Stonehouse was tracked down to Victoria and charged on Christmas Eve by Melbourne police (who happened to be looking for that other recent high-profile fugitive from justice, Lord Lucan) with entering the country using a false passport. That image of a pile of clothes on a beach as a signifier of a faked suicide fed in (completely coincidentally, it seems) to the premise for the popular 1970s British sitcom *The Fall and Rise of Reginald Perrin*, written by David Nobbs. Perrin (played by Leonard Rossiter, *2001*'s Dr. Andrei Smyslov) a 46-year-old advertising executive, sick of his occupation and dreary middle class suburban life, who decides to orchestrate his own demise and assume a fresh identity. In the factual and fictional cases of Stonehouse and Perrin, their efforts failed. The final episode of the sitcom, entitled 'Full Circle', finds Perrin, having passed through various phases of reinvention, returned to a life not unlike the one he was determined to escape from right at the very beginning of his odyssey. Once again he contemplates the beach. By returning to the sands of Malibu in the final few seconds of *Seconds*, there is the suggestion that this location, like the recycling of experience for Company clients, is destined to be stuck on repeat.

Long before *Seconds*, an Irish song called 'Michael Finnegan' (supposedly first documented in *The Hackney Scout Song Book* in 1921 but origins unknown) commits its titular character to a rinse-repeat cycle that continues for as long as the singers of the song deem it necessary. It is an example of an unboundedly long song or repetitive song, a style of song that is common in many global cultures, including the Caribbean and Southern India, but also frequently associated with children or the African American slave culture as a means of wiling away time and/or making that which is intolerable more bearable. In 'Michael Finnegan' – an old man with whiskers on his 'chin-igan' – the verses refer to mundane and insubstantial details of Finnegan's life that invariably come to an unfortunate resolution before he's forced to 'begin-again'.

There was an old man called Michael Finn-egan,
He grew whiskers on his chin-igan,
The wind came up and blew them in-again,
Poor old Michael Finnegan. Begin-again.

There was an old man called Michael Finn-egan,
He kicked up an awful din-igan.
Because they said he must not sing again.
Poor old Michael Finnegan. Begin-again.

There was an old man called Michael Finn-egan,
Ran a race and tried to win again.
Got so puffed that he had to go in again.
Poor old Michael Finnegan. Begin-again.

While there is a stock-standard roster of lyrics associated with Michael Finnegan, it is ostensibly up to the singer to fill the blanks as they see fit, coming up with their own shenanigans for Finnegan before he then begins again. The details are not important; what is important is that Finnegan is subjected to this infinite cycle, this treadmill of life, through which he is unable to escape, at least for as long as the song is sung.

In *Seconds*, despite his misfortunes, Hamilton/Wilson is committed to 'begin again' and it is the Company that eventually dictates his end. For all the hopelessness of Hamilton/Wilson and the film itself, he still does not give up hope of achieving a better life or the possibility that he will be successful in his pursuit of happiness if he's just allowed to 'begin again'. We've talked about *Seconds* having no hope but Hamilton/Wilson's continued drive to thrive and not to give up is symptomatic of the human biological imperative to survive. Even in the face of defeat, Hamilton/Wilson refuses to surrender, which could be naivety, foolishness or courage, depending on the viewer's own outlook. However, it is hard to see this as cause for hope within the context of a film that gives us so little. As human beings, while we are all fated to the same end with work and consumption filling the gaps between birth and death, there is a tendency to believe the 'grass is always greener' if we could only be... insert wish here. In *Seconds*, the Hamilton/Wilson amalgam gets to do what we can only figuratively do: walk in someone else's shoes.

Notes

1. Some accounts suggest that also present as dinner guests at the residence on the evening of 3rd June 1968 along with Robert Kennedy were Roman Polanski and Sharon Tate. The Malibu Colony beach house is around a forty-minute journey from Cielo Drive where, a little over 14 months later, Tate would be murdered along with three other associates by members of the Manson Family.
2. Edward Lewis' 2019 obituary in *The Washington Post* pays tribute to the part he played in breaking the blacklist, specifically in crediting Dalton Trumbo as the screenwriter of *Spartacus*: https://www.washingtonpost.com/local/obituaries/edward-lewis-spartacus-producer-who-helped-break-the-blacklist-dies-at-99/2019/08/13/9e9be300-bdd9-11e9-b873-63ace636af08_story.html

LASTS: 'Relax, old friend. Cranial drill'

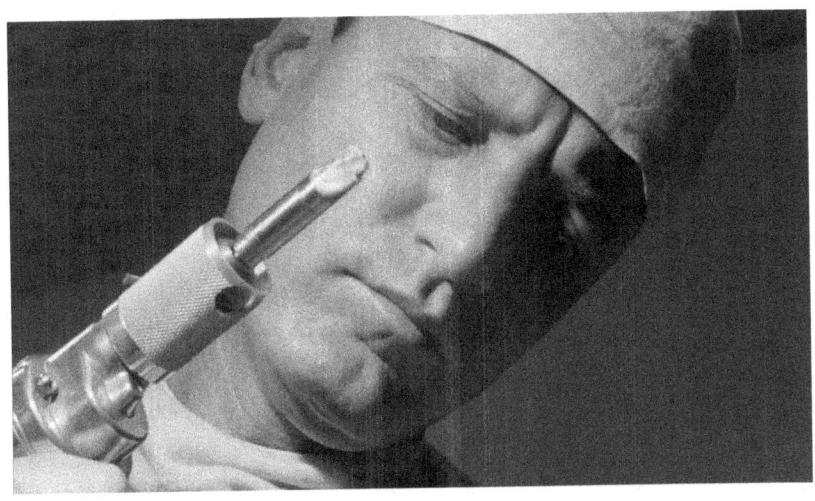

I looked upon the sea. It was to be my grave. – Mary Shelley, *Frankenstein, or, the modern prometheus*.

Seconds ends with a beginning. We see a man, not he who was once Arthur Hamilton, perhaps his former acquaintance, seemingly living the life that the Company promised him. His dream come true. Maybe this time it will work out and there will be no need to recall this Reborn and put him through 'the next stage' of processing for the benefit of some other Company client, surgically rendered to mimic the result of an automobile accident or a hunting misadventure or a hotel room fire, courtesy of the Cadaver Procurement Section. Somehow though, through the curved distortion of those very final frames, we must doubt that there is ever likely to be a happy outcome for anyone entering into a Company contract. In the absence of hope we are left to hold on to the film as a warning, one that we can choose to apply to the decisions that we make in our daily lives. Through this reception and appreciation of the film we are able to make it personal, if not altogether palatable. So it was for its star.

According to *Rock Hudson: His Story*, the book that Hudson collaborated on with Sara

Davidson as a final and partly post-mortem record of his frequently misrepresented life, the actor met with Stockton Briggle, film producer and friend, in the autumn of 1982, about a year after the emergency quintuple bypass surgery that saved his life following a heart attack. Surviving this trauma, he mused to Briggle:

> 'It's time to make my own decisions, my own choices. It's time to do what I want to do without other people running my life.' (Hudson/Davidson 2007:162)

It is a matter of record that throughout the years that followed the film's release, Hudson considered *Seconds* to be among his finest work, and he continued to defend it and his performance despite the film failing to find favour in the court of critical opinion. It was a championing that he maintained despite the film marking the moment of his career downturn. Remaining so loyal to a piece of work so roundly considered to be a failure must indicate that it retained a highly personal significance for the actor, perhaps as a telling, if harrowing, allegory of his own life.

In a procedure that comes close to some kind of cinematic pathology, the authors have both been drawn to run a magnifying glass over the corpse of *Seconds*, and in the process we hope to have at least partially revived the film for the purposes of a wider appreciation. For anyone either resisting the experience of watching the film based on its notorious reception, or otherwise resolute in their antipathy towards it, we would simply encourage you to put aside your preconceptions or prejudices, relax and let it open up your head. Tony Wilson's last words in the original David Ely novel, as he succumbs to the anaesthetic prior to his terminal operation, speak of a tranquil(ised), if defeated, finality: 'It really doesn't matter.' As an artifact of personal enrichment, in the case of *Seconds* the film, we beg to differ.

BIBLIOGRAPHY

Books

BASS, J., & KIRKHAM, P. (2011). *Saul Bass: a life in film & design*. London, Laurence King Pub.

BOYLE, F. (2012). *Work! Consume! Die!* London, HarperCollins.

CARROLL, L. (2003). *Alice's adventures in Wonderland and Through the looking-glass and what Alice found there. Introduction and notes by Hugh Haughton*. London, Penguin.

HUDSON, R., & DAVIDSON, S. (2007). *Rock Hudson: his story*. New York, Carroll & Graf.

ELY, D. (1963). *Seconds: a novel.* New York, Pantheon Books.

EPPRIDGE, B. (2008). *A time it was: Bobby Kennedy in the Sixties*. New York, Abrams., excerpts sourced online from Today. 4 June https://www.today.com/popculture/journalist-captures-bobby-kennedy-sixties-1C9017434

JUAN, & BYRON, G. G. B. (1822). *[Don Juan. Cantos III. IV and V.]*. London, Thomas Davison.

MOLDEA, D. E. (2018). *The killing of Robert F. Kennedy: an investigation of motive, means, and opportunity.*, excerpts sourced online https://www.moldea.com/rfk.html

PASTOURMATZI, D. (2002). *Biotechnological and medical themes in science fiction*. Thessaloniki, University Studio Press.

POMERANCE, M., & PALMER, R. B. (2011). *A little solitaire: John Frankenheimer and American film*. New Brunswick, N.J., Rutgers University Press.

PRATLEY, G. (1969). *The cinema of John Frankenheimer*. London, Zwemmer.

SHELLEY, M. W. (2003) *Frankenstein, or, the modern prometheus*. Rev. edn. Edited by M. Hindle. London: Penguin Books (Penguin Classics).

WILSON, B., & GOLD, T. (1991). *Wouldn't it be nice: my own story*. New York, NY, Harper Collins.

Articles, online and other sources

Amram, D., 'The Manchurian Candidate' https://www.davidamram.com/manchurian.html

Anderson, M., 2013. 'Face Off' Artforum. 12 August https://www.artforum.com/film/melissa-anderson-on-john-frankenheimer-s-seconds 42364

Axelman, A., 2011. 'Fallen Under the Radar — My Resurrection of John Frankenheimer' [online] The Wrap https://www.thewrap.com/fallen-under-radar-my-resurrectuion-john-frankenheimer-32906/

Babb, S., 1928-2005. 'Sanora Babb: An Inventory of Her Papers in the Manuscript Collection at the Harry Ransom Center' Henry Ransom Center, University of Texas at Austin. https://norman.hrc.utexas.edu/fasearch/findingAid.cfm?eadid=00501

Barsanti, C., 2013. 'There Are No Second Chances in Seconds' Popmatters. 29 August https://www.popmatters.com/174688-seconds-this-is-your-life-2495730274.html

Barson, M. 'John Frankenheimer: American Director' Britannica.com https://www.britannica.com/biography/John-Frankenheimer

Baxter, B., 2002. 'John Frankenheimer' *The Guardian* UK. 8 July https://www.theguardian.com/news/2002/jul/08/guardianobituaries.booksobituaries

Easton, S., 2012. 'The Old Vines Are Buried Deep: Classical Motifs in John Frankenheimer's Seconds' *Illinois Classical Studies*, No. 37 https://www.jstor.org/stable/10.5406/illiclasstud.37.0199

Engle, Gary D. and John Frankenheimer. 'John Frankenheimer: An Interview.' *Film Criticism*, vol. 2, no. 1, 1977, pp. 2–14. JSTOR, www.jstor.org/stable/44019037 (Accessed 22 February 2021).

Farber, S., 1966-67. 'Seconds by John Frankenheimer' *Film Quarterly*, Vol. 20, No. 2 pp. 25-28, https://www.jstor.org/stable/1210691

Frankenheimer, J. *Seconds* audio commentary, DVD, [New York]: The Criterion Collection, [2013] ©1966.

Franklin, C., 2006. 'Bobby misses haunting stories' *Chicago Tribune*. https://www.

chicagotribune.com/news/ct-xpm-2006-11-30-0611300038-story.html

Kahlenberg, Richard D., 2018. 'The Inclusive Populism of Robert F. Kennedy' The Century Foundation. 16 March https://tcf.org/content/report/inclusive-populism-robert-f-kennedy/?agreed=1&agreed=1

LoBrutto, V., 2018. 'The Surreal Images of Seconds' *American Cinematographer*. 31 January https://ascmag.com/articles/the-surreal-images-of-seconds

Maiuro, T., 2013. 'Seconds' Cineaste. November.

McLean, R., 2015. 'Cult Movie: Seconds a bad trip in film form' The Irish News. 13 November https://www.irishnews.com/arts/2015/11/13/news/cult-movie-seconds-a-bad-trip-in-film-form-321281/

McLeod, S. A., 2018. *Visual perception theory*. Simply Psychology. https://www.simplypsychology.org/perception-theories.html

Pelan, T., 'Limitation of Life: You can't go back in John Frankenheimer's Seconds' Cinephilia & Beyond. https://cinephiliabeyond.org/limitation-life-cant-go-back-john-frankenheimers-seconds/

Phelps, D., 1993. 'Faces' *Film Comment* p. 72. March.

Rusch, K.K., 1994. 'Seconds' The Magazine of Fantasy and Science Fiction. January http://www.sfsite.com/fsf/

Satuloff, B., 1997. 'Seconds' The Advocate. 13 May http://www.advocate.com/

Sterritt, D., 2013. 'Seconds: Reborn Again' Criterion.com. 13 August https://www.criterion.com/current/posts/2867-seconds-reborn-again

Smith, H., 2019. 'Edward Lewis, Spartacus producer who helped break the blacklist, dies at 99' The Washington Post. 14 August https://www.washingtonpost.com/local/obituaries/edward-lewis-spartacus-producer-who-helped-break-the-blacklist-dies-at-99/2019/08/13/9e9be300-bdd9-11e9-b873-63ace636af08_story.html

Tenner, E., 2013. 'A Second Life for Seconds, the 1966 Cult Classic That Made Audiences Sick' The Atlantic. 22 August https://www.theatlantic.com/entertainment/archive/2013/08/a-second-life-for-em-seconds-em-the-1966-cult-classic-that-made-audiences-sick/278930/

Weinraub, B., 2002. 'John Frankenheimer is Dead at 72' New York Times. 8 July https://www.nytimes.com/2002/07/08/movies/john-frankenheimer-dead-72-resilient-director-feature-films-tv-movies.html?auth=login-facebook

Willens, M., 2017. 'The Rise of the Malibu Movie Colony' Daily Beast. 12 July https://www.thedailybeast.com/the-rise-of-the-malibu-movie-colony

Wiltshire, P., 2001. 'A Key Unturned: Seconds' Senses of Cinema, Issue 18. December http://sensesofcinema.com/2001/underrated-and-overlooked/seconds/

Filmed resources

Fear Itself (dir. Charlie Lyne, 2015) BBC Films. Available via BBC iPlayer (viewed 18 October 2015).

Rock Hudson – Making of *Seconds* – 1965 https://www.youtube.com/watch?v=1OzjQAQJ6Zc&feature=youtu.be

'Rock Hudson: Acting the Part' (1999) Biography. A&E, 7 March https://www.dailymotion.com/video/x3dbacu

Seconds, DVD, [New York]: The Criterion Collection, [2013] ©1966.

Seconds, 'Masters of Cinema' dual format (Blu-ray & DVD), Eureka Entertainment, [2015] ©1966.

Constellations

'This stunning, sharp series of books fills a real need for authoritative, compact studies of key science fiction films. ...the volumes in the Constellations series promise to set the standard for SF film studies in the 21st century.' Wheeler Winston Dixon, Ryan Professor of Film Studies, University of Nebraska

Children of Men – Dan Dinello

"...an impressive, intelligent and perceptive analysis of a film increasingly recognised in retrospect as a classic of modern dystopian cinema." Starburst

Close Encounters of the Third Kind – Jon Towlson

"...a thoroughly researched, lucid, and insightful study that succeeds on multiple levels of inquiry." Extrapolation

Ex Machina – Joshua Grimm

Exploring Ex Machina's *ideas about consciousness, embodiment, and masculinity, all through the lens of a misogynist mad scientist, Joshua Grimm argues the result is a fascinating and unique film that immediately established Alex Garland as a breakout voice in the landscape of science fiction film.*

Robocop – Omar Ahmed

"...this exceptional monograph... is essential reading for sf and film critics as well as fans who are nostalgic for an era that marked the end of sf as a genuine art form." Extrapolation

www.ingramcontent.com/pod-product-compliance
Lightning Source LLC
Chambersburg PA
CBHW071413300426
44114CB00016B/2288